Metadata for Content Management

Designing taxonomy, metadata, policy and workflow to make
digital content systems better for users.

By David Diamond

Contact the author:

david@ContentManagementBook.com

linkedin.com/in/airdiamond

Twitter: @DAMSurvival

ContentManagementBook.com

CreateSpace Edition
July, 2016 (v1.1)

Table of Contents

Intro

A good content management system (CMS) or digital asset management (DAM) system with a bad taxonomy or metadata schema design is virtually indistinguishable from a bad system.

There are many factors that play into whether a system ends up being a true asset to an organization, but at the core of most content systems that fail is poor taxonomy and metadata schema design, a lack of clear and sustainable policy, or both.

Granted, software limitations can limit your potential to do what you need; but in too many cases, the system's full potential is never realized because the taxonomy and metadata design has never been given the consideration it deserves.

This book aims to help you think more clearly about how taxonomy, metadata can be used within the limitations and advantages of content management systems, and how policy and workflow can help keep the system clean and running smoothly.

The lines between DAM, CMS, enterprise content management (ECM) systems, brand asset management (BAM) systems and all the rest increasingly blur over time, so I refer to all of it when I write *content system*. It's all digital content and most management concepts apply to each class equally.

And when I write *content management system*, I don't mean just *Web* content management systems, systems like WordPress; I mean any system designed to manage any type of digital content.

I don't expect any recognizable separation between these various terms and software classes to last much longer—they are all on a collision course toward becoming the same thing. It won't be long before the only differentiation between content systems comes from specific features. Some will continue to be better suited toward one type of content management than another, but they will all be content management systems.

Some people will fight to try to retain separation between these terms and technologies, likely because they're trying to justify some niche (limitation) of the software they sell.

I am not one of those people. I say let's recognize that these previously diverse systems are becoming more alike than ever. By continuing to support increasingly-difficult-to-justify class differences, we continue to confuse the discussion.

Whether we speak of images, layouts, audio, website pages, logos, annual reports, documentation, policy definitions, brand messaging, social media posts or anything else of that nature, we speak of the management of content.

So let's call it what it is: *content management*.

I have no background in Library Science, so nothing in this book will be presented from that or any other perspective that's not based on my own personal experiences. If you can understand the words you're reading now, you'll be able to understand all concepts presented herein.

If you're interested in learning more about the basics of digital asset management from a more traditional "DAM" perspective, my book, *DAM Survival Guide*, is a good place to start. It offers a more general overview of the subject that I think might help you get even more out of the book you're now reading.

Consider *Metadata for Content Management* a good fit for you if:

- You are certain that some sort of system for managing digital content is what your organization needs, and you can envision how the system will help make things better
- You're looking for a bridge between academic discussions of taxonomy, metadata and policy, and real-world applications that relate specifically to content management

As with *DAM Survival Guide*, you will find no system software recommendations in this book. Instead, my primary aim is to help you understand how you'll use taxonomy and metadata so when you are considering new content software, you can more quickly and reliably recognize deal-breaker system limitations when you see them.

If you're already set up with content software, my hope is that this book will enable you to better understand what limitations you'll face as you try to make that software work. You might have to reduce your expectations or you might need different software. Either way, better you know up front, before you waste countless hours trying to make a system do what it wasn't designed to do.

If you take away one thing from this book, let it be this:

The primary purpose of content management software is to enable you to manage taxonomy and metadata, which, in turn, are the controls that make the management of digital content possible. If taxonomy and metadata aren't considered carefully, you can assume your content management initiative will become just another significant cost item that yields no appreciable return.

What Made the Content System so Bad?

When we buy things, we want them to just work. We want no hassles and we want no downtime spent reading instructions or calling support lines. In fact, there is such a trend in software development toward user friendliness and sexy user experience—fueled mainly by the focused simplicity of mobile apps—that the enterprise software industry finds itself scrambling to figure out how to serve massive complexity through UIs that offer only a few widgets.

This is good and bad.

When it comes to content management software, "off the shelf" readiness simply means the system comes preconfigured to perfectly suit no one. It's akin to some drug being marketed as "effective for curing things." Sometimes things just aren't simple. Managing content is about defining and adhering to policy, routing and tracking it all.

If you can envision a simple app that will do all this, the content software industry is waiting for you to own it.

Configuration is key for content software efficacy. In fact, the very same software heralded as a godsend by one customer can be cursed as a nightmare by another, simply because of the differences in the way the system was configured or is used.

Unfortunately, too many content systems are ill-configured or ill-suited for their intended purposes. It would be easy to blame software salespeople for leading customers astray, but there is a significant amount of responsibility here that lies squarely on the shoulders of the purchaser. The Toyota Prius owner who commutes a hundred miles per day is going to love her car much more than the Toyota Prius owner who gets stuck in the mud every time he goes off-roading.

While the similarities between content management systems are greater than the differences, being able to choose the best system for your needs and goals lies in your ability to determine which system can most effectively and easily do what you need it to do. This, in turn, means you must be able to define those needs with some precision so that you'll know when a system you're considering (or have already purchased) is up to the task.

This is where taxonomy and metadata design come into the picture. Taxonomy and metadata are the basis for how content is tagged, categorized, found, valued, licensed, moved through productions, etc. While there are many other important aspects to system configuration, such as access permissions, user and group accounts, content processing configurations and more, virtually all of these considerations are secondary to how your core taxonomy and metadata schemas are designed and managed.

If your system can't support the taxonomy and metadata schema models you need, it's not going to work for you. It doesn't mean you have a bad system, but it will considered a bad system by your users if you can't configure it as it should be configured to suit your organization's policies and workflow requirements.

Keep this in mind as you read through the remainder of this book. Forget what your content system can do now, and forget what software vendors promise their software can ultimately do. From this point on, think entirely in terms of the *organization of content*. With a handle on how you want to accomplish that, you'll know exactly what you need from your software.

Taxonomy, Metadata, Tags and Controlled Vocabularies

Let's review some simplified definitions:

- Taxonomy – A collection of terms that are organized into some structure that provides some semantic understanding of those terms. (For example, where "Turkey" falls beneath "Food" in a hierarchy, it's presumed to be about the cooked dish, not the live bird, country or bowling triumph.)
- Metadata – Terms, numeric values or any other information that describes a piece of content's status, location, physical attributes, etc.
- Tags – Terms that are assigned to content to help identify that content. Tags are often applied without semantic or hierarchical consideration.
- Controlled Vocabularies – A collection of standardized or agreed upon terms that are used to identify content.

Now take another look at those definitions. If you're thinking they all sound pretty much the same, you are correct. A tag is just a term (word or phrase). A vocabulary is made up of multiple terms. A taxonomy is tree-like structure that provides some semantic understanding of the terms it contains. And metadata is the word we use to describe all of it.

Any software-specific differences that exist between these various metadata concepts come entirely from how each is used within the configuration and use of the system.

The Software System Perspective

When we look at these metadata concepts through the eyes of a content management interface, we gain some clarity on how each fits into the bigger picture.

The taxonomy tree

Many content systems include a tree-like structure that enables terms to be organized into hierarchies. Users can drag and drop content onto the terms (or vice versa) to make assignments. This is how most systems present taxonomies to users. It's a fairly intuitive means for viewing and working with a taxonomy, but such a hierarchical representation of terms presents drawbacks too, which are discussed later.

⊞ Expertise

⊞ Industries

⊟ Languages

    Arabic

    English

    French

    German

    Hindi

    Italian

    Japanese

    Korean

This simple taxonomy includes branches (nodes) for Expertise, Industries and Languages. Some content systems enable you to use taxonomy nodes as input filters for metadata fields, as shown below.

Field filters as controlled vocabularies

When branches (or nodes) of a taxonomy are assigned as input filters to specific metadata fields, they serve as controlled vocabularies. When a field is configured as such, only those terms in the assigned branch can be entered into the metadata field; terms not found in the vocabulary branch are rejected.

The Languages node of the taxonomy shown above has been assigned as an input filter for this field. Only terms found in that branch of the taxonomy are accepted into the field; other terms would be rejected. As the user types "Ger…" the word "German" appears as a suggestion.

Some systems also enable users to create lists that are used in the same way: a list of terms is created (or subscribed to as an external resource), and the terms in that list become the allowable values for any metadata field to which the list has been assigned. In these cases, the lists might be completely disconnected from any taxonomy.

Tags

In some systems, users can simply enter terms that then become system-wide tags. The system remembers which tags have been used before, and it offers them as suggestions in the future. This could be considered an "uncontrolled" vocabulary in that it doesn't restrict what can be entered, whether the values are accurate or not.

Some systems require that tags be provided by a node in the taxonomy tree or a predefined list of terms, essentially making the concept of controlled vocabulary input and tagging input identical.

Metadata schema

The entire array of available metadata fields is considered the system's *metadata schema*. In most DAMs, metadata schemas are static, meaning that the same set of fields is available across all content.

Adaptive metadata schemas make it possible for each piece of content in a system to have its own metadata schema, if required. As of this writing, Picturepark is the only content system I know of at the time of this writing that offers this capability; but other vendors can be expected to follow suit because of the potential this new metadata paradigm offers.

If you're in the market for content software, ask the vendors you speak to if they support multiple or layered metadata schemas, or plan to in the future. They might offer the feature using a different name than adaptive metadata. Just make sure what is offered is truly about enabling you to define different classes of content, and not just that they do something as simple as change available metadata fields based on the file format of the underlying content. For example, a logo, product box photo or a CEO headshot might all be JPG files, but their metadata needs are dramatically different.

Location vs. attributes

Understanding that vocabularies, tags and taxonomies are all just metadata makes it easier *and* more difficult to explain their differences to users. In order to simplify the discussion, I explain it like this:

Taxonomy terms, like folders in a file cabinet, are locations into which digital content can be classified. Vocabularies and tags are attributes that are assigned to that content.

Admittedly, this perspective is based entirely on the user experience provided by content systems. Meaning, for example, that I can drag and drop content onto taxonomy terms, which "feels" like I'm putting them there. By contrast, when I'm adding tags inside a metadata editing window, it feels like I'm adding attributes.

In fact, both operations are exactly the same, particularly when controlled vocabulary terms come from the taxonomy.

But because these concepts are derived from the physical world, we have to consider that perspective when discussing the concepts with others. For example, the folders in a file cabinet are locations into which we put documents (taxonomy), while the "PAID" and other stamps we put on those documents are attributes (tags).

For many, it's too tempting to not borrow real-world concepts when configuring a CMS or DAM, which is fine in many cases. Just keep in mind that any such definitions you adopt for your system are purely academic— it's all metadata.

Content System Advantages

Taxonomy design for content management isn't exactly like traditional taxonomy design. Computers are more flexible than library shelves. Digital content *can* be in two (or more) places at once. Further, the ability to find content based on taxonomy facets, means that deeply nested taxonomies are far less often required.

Consider the following hierarchical structure:

```
Content

↳ 2015

      ↳ Marketing

             ↳ Advertising

                   ↳ Products

                   ↳ Services
```

This structure is understandable, once it's been explained. "We organize content by year, then department, then type, then…"

While this structure might be convenient for some users, other users would see it as a hindrance. For example, someone in Marketing might resent having to always navigate through year categories in order to see the Marketing content. Someone else might have a need for advertising materials from some year unknown.

What makes hierarchical organization like this even worse is that with each new year, the entire substructure needs to be created anew.

By contrast, faceted organization enables you to remove the hierarchical requirements and achieve even more flexible (and obvious) results to users. By clicking relevant checkboxes, users narrow in on the results they need, often without any knowledge of the greater taxonomy. If a facet isn't relevant for a given search, it can be ignored. (For example, maybe the year isn't important.)

Below is the taxonomy above (with additional options) presented in a faceted model. Most invisibly relevant about this model is that it requires virtually no training. Faceted taxonomies invite users to experiment, whereas clicking in and out through hierarchical taxonomies quickly becomes tiresome and frustrating. (It can also be difficult to remember which branches of the tree you've already visited.)

```
Year

↳ 2015

↳ 2014

Department

↳ Marketing

↳ Support

Type

↳ Advertising

        ↳ Product

        ↳ Services
```

When using a faceted taxonomy approach, only a single new tag will be required for each new year, new department or new content type.

What does need to be considered is the "and/or" aspect of each facet. For example, if 2014 and 2015 were both selected in the example above, it means either "find assets created in *either* 2014 or 2015" or "find assets created in *both* 2014 and 2015."

Some content systems don't offer both options, meaning their facets are always either "and" or "or," which can confuse users. For example, someone expecting to see assets from either year (or) might see nothing when selecting both options because no asset was developed in both years (and).

This, of course, is a user experience issue. It's perfectly possible for a system to indicate which Boolean function is being considered within a faceted group. The challenge might be finding a system whose designers understood the value in doing so.

When designing taxonomies for physical objects and spaces, faceting is not an option. But when designing for CMS or digital asset management systems, it's important to think about all the advantages available.

Taxonomy Design from Scratch

We all know bad organization when we see it. Yet, when charged with creating a good taxonomy, we realize it's not as easy as it might seem.

Aside from taxonomists and information professionals who have been trained in the art of taxonomy design, there aren't many individuals who can build a usable taxonomy from scratch—at least not at first try. Taxonomy design for content management has a lot to do with imagining how people think, anticipating and delivering what they expect, and predicting the future.

Among the more common obstacles that face the newbie taxonomist is the realization that not everyone thinks the same way. What seems obvious to the taxonomy designer might seem downright mysterious to others. This is why user interviews and institutional research are so important when creating a taxonomy that will be used across an organization.

Fortunately, in some cases what's obvious to one will be obvious to all. This enables you to get started with a concept without undue delay. But make sure you don't get too far without pulling others into the conversation.

Let's look at how we might develop a simple content management taxonomy from scratch.

Consider the following tags:

```
horse, cake, car, flower
```

These terms could be applied directly to a content as metadata tags that describe the content. But imagine you needed some more granularity than just these four tags. Imagine you needed the flexibility to tag all animal species, all food products made by a given manufacturer, all auto brands, or a few thousand types of flowers.

Upon collecting these thousands of terms, your instinct would likely be to organize them in some way. At the very least, you'd separate the terms into headings like "Animals" and "Food" and "Autos" and "Flowers."

But you'd likely go further than that. You might alphabetize the terms and even subcategorize them so that they'd be easier to manage. Animals might be split into mammals, reptiles, etc. Food products might be categorized by type, such as dairy, meats, canned goods, etc. Your auto tags might be split into luxury or sports or even European or Japanese subcategories. And all those flowers terms could be classified by color, season or even scientific name.

In fact, in what you're doing when organizing tags is building a taxonomy. Recalling our definition that states that a taxonomy is a structure that provides some semantic understanding of the terms it contains, those category headings you'd be adding are the basis for that semantic understanding. The "Animals" heading, for example, will disambiguate the "Mustang" horse tag from its namesake muscle car.

Envision Organization

When you initially organized your filing cabinet at home, was your goal to have a place to *put* things, or to have a place from where you can easily *get* things?

The distinction is important because it speaks to motivation.

For example, if your goal was to merely have a place to store physical documents, you didn't likely think too much about how the cabinet was organized. You might have put all tax documents into a single folder, without thinking about tax year. Or you might have created another folder for all receipts, without thinking about which you'll need come tax season.

Alphabetization was likely your default option for ordering the folders themselves because, why not? But does it make sense for the A, B and C folders to be more readily accessible than the R, S, and T folders?

On the other hand, if your goal was easy retrieval, you likely put yourself in the mental space of having an immediate need for those files. What will I be doing when I need something? Paying bills? Doing my tax return? Where would I expect to find property tax documents about the house: Under "House Files" or "Tax Documents"?

Considering immediate need is how we organize our kitchens and (physical) desktops. We think in terms of what we'll need when, rather than what something is called.

A complexity about designing a content system is that, ideally, you offer both options—some ordered means of storage, such as alphabetization, plus a more "immediate need" option too. This enables users to easily find new and popular content, while they can rely on archives being in some order that can be learned and relied upon.

As difficult as it is to think in terms of how you'd personally expect to find things, it can be even more difficult to imagine how others will expect to find what they need. If someone else set up your filing cabinet in accordance with his or her expectations, you might have already experienced some confusion or frustration when you've tried to find things.

Real-world Taxonomy Examples

One place where we're all at the mercy of someone else's taxonomy design is the grocery store. When you walk into a new store, consider the first thing you do: You might stop, look around and try to get a visual sense of the store based on signage. Or, if you're more interested in quickly finding what you need than in learning about the store, you might ask someone to point you in the right direction.

The next time you walk down a grocery store aisle, consider how things are grouped. This is a taxonomy of products, even if it does or does not make sense to you. For example, there might be a special section for Asian foods, but this isn't where you'll find rice. Vegetables and meats are popular in Asian cooking too, but they'll also be located elsewhere.

When you consider that rice, vegetables and meat are also used in other cuisines, you can understand the decision to not put them in the Asian food section. But it's important to note that your understanding comes not from knowledge about the grocery store taxonomy, but from your own understanding of how foods are used.

In theory, a grocery store should be accessible to anyone, regardless of his or her ability to cook or understand international cuisine. In fact, grocery store taxonomists make assumptions about customer knowledge, and most of those assumptions are based on having an understanding of food.

This means it's the people who *don't* cook who typically spend the most time trying to find the basics. These people have no backgrounds from which to make sense of a grocery store's layout (taxonomy). In time, they learn where things are; but if you ask them why something is found in one place over another, chances are they will have no idea.

You'll also experience taxonomy on websites. The very organization of content on each site is a taxonomy. As a user of these sites, you might have already made some judgements about which sites are good and bad.

For example, maybe while looking for technical support information for your mobile phone, you had to sift through pages and pages of content about washing machines and vacuum cleaners. From the manufacturer's perspective, a single "everything" support site might make perfect sense. But from your "user in need" perspective, completeness was nothing more than an inconvenience. And when presented in the form of taxonomical organization, it just seemed overwhelming.

Amazon.com provides another good example. From the US Amazon website, you can order more than 300 million products, each categorized into a standard taxonomy. Yet, you probably don't even rely on that taxonomy when buying products because you've found you can't rely on it. Instead, you likely search for keywords and browse the results.

A similar case was early Yahoo!, which started out as a directory of Internet content. It might have made total sense at the time to classify the world's content into browsable categories, but Google saw how that wasn't going to be sustainable—there was just too much content and too many categories for it be manageable or even understandable by users. When you visit Google, you're offered no taxonomy at all. And yet, it's somehow the best Internet search option we have.

People use content systems much like they use grocery stores, websites and search engines. Some are willing to spend time browsing the system to see what's available, while others come to the system in need of something specific.

If you provide a good taxonomy, users unfamiliar with the system should be able to find what they need without assistance. But if what you offer is too complex, it won't help anyone.

In most cases, no matter how well conceived your taxonomy, users must become familiar with "the store" before they become productive because there will always be certain organizational decisions, like religious candles being shelved beside the Mexican specialty foods, that we just have to learn and accept. Where else would you stock these candles in a food store? (And why are candles even in a food store?)

So when envisioning your taxonomy, don't think in terms of perfection. Instead, think in terms of how people are most likely to find things based on what they already know and expect. Building a taxonomy is not about educating and changing perspectives; it's about leveraging existing perspectives with the aim of providing an intuitive experience.

Determine Your Terms

If you're developing a taxonomy for your organization, chances are there is some corporate or industrial vocabulary that can serve as a foundation for your taxonomy. Even if an institutional vocabulary isn't known to you (or anyone else), you can begin to derive a taxonomy by listening to conversations. For example, you might not know a thing about aviation, but that won't stop you from creating a taxonomy for aviation purposes.

Let's give it a try:

Good evening ladies and gentleman, this is your pilot, Nancy Jetson, speaking from the cockpit. On behalf of first officer, Randy Rudder, I'd like to welcome you aboard this Taxonomy Airways Boeing 777. We'll be flying at an altitude of 35,000 feet today en route to Toronto. The weather in Toronto today is cold, with light snow showers. Once we're airborne, our flight attendants will come through the cabin to offer you a beverage. Passengers in First Class can enjoy our in-seat entertainment system. Passengers seated in the main cabin can entertain yourselves by kicking the seat in front of you. As a reminder, please remain seated with your seat belts fastened during taxi, takeoff and landing. Federal regulations forbid congregating outside the forward lavatories near the cockpit.

Without knowing a thing about aviation, we can derive some taxonomy from this speech:

Departure Times
  ↳ Evening
Destinations
  ↳ Toronto
Crew Positions
  ↳ Pilot
  ↳ First Officer
  ↳ Flight Attendant
Aircraft Type
  ↳ Boeing 777
Flight Altitudes
  ↳ 35,000 feet
Weather Conditions
  ↳ Cold
  ↳ Snow Showers
Phases of Flight
  ↳ Airborne
  ↳ Taxiing
  ↳ Takeoff
  ↳ Landing
Airplane Sections
  ↳ First Class
  ↳ Main Cabin
  ↳ Cockpit
  ↳ Lavatories

While incomplete, this provides us with some useful information we can use to fill in some blanks. For example, what other destinations do we serve?

What other times of the day do we depart? Is it always cold and snowy at our destinations? Do we always fly at 35,000 feet?

Based on supplied or known values, you can presume optional values. Your subject matter experts can then confirm which values make sense. For example, does a cruising altitude of 40,000 feet make sense? What about 100 or 100,000 feet? Even if you don't know these answers, someone will.

It will be your job as the taxonomist to determine a topics structure that works for your organization, even if no one has ever considered one before. Listen to what's going on around you and ask questions.

Determine the Scope of Your Terms

Though we aren't bound in digital asset management by the limitations of hierarchical taxonomy, it's natural for us to think in terms of hierarchy when organizing our terms. Part of this consideration is the scope of the taxonomy, or how deep in either direction the hierarchy should go.

For example, if your content system houses only photos of the farming equipment you manufacture, you know that your outer terms—the ones at the top of your taxonomy hierarchy—needn't extend beyond that equipment. The following might make sense:

```
Tractors
        ↳ Model 100
        ↳ Model 200
Backhoe
        ↳ Model 1211
        ↳ Model 1455
```

By contrast, this "more complete" taxonomy would not make sense:

```
Objects
     ↳ Vehicles
          ↳ Air
          ↳ Space
          ↳ Sea
          ↳ Land
               ↳ Farming
                    Tractors
                    ↳ Model 100
                    ↳ Model 200
                    Backhoe
                         ↳ Model 1211
                         ↳ Model 1455
```

The scope of this taxonomy is much too wide for its intended purpose. There are those who would argue that a taxonomy should provide room for future expansion, and this is a good point. But only you and your company experts will be able to determine whether your current farm equipment focus is likely to expand to include vehicles for space travel.

The detailed side of the taxonomy (inner sub terms) can be more difficult to trim. This is also where you might find the most argument from your users. For example, your Model 100 tractor might come in 5 colors. Do you need subcategories for color? That will depend on what you intend to have in your system and how many assets you expect to be managing.

For example, if you assume there will be only two photos of each tractor in each color, that's only 10 photos that would be assigned to the Model 100 tag. That wouldn't overwhelm users. And something as obvious in a photo as color might require no categorization anyway.

If color is an important consideration, it could be another node within your taxonomy. Using faceted search, users could use the same color choices for multiple vehicles.

```
Tractors
        ↳ Model 100

        ↳ Model 200

Backhoe
        ↳ Model 1211

        ↳ Model 1455

Colors
        ↳ Glorious Green

        ↳ Radical Red

        ↳ Outrageous Orange

        ↳ Ballistic Blue
```

If you're not the subject matter expert (SME) for your organization or field, find that person. An SME can help you determine a reasonable scope for your taxonomy. But keep in mind that even the most experienced experts might not be able to provide a scope that makes total sense. Expertise tends to favor the complete, while usability favors the fast and easy. Interview experts and then take your findings and assumptions to the users to make sure everyone sees things the same way.

Outward from the Root

It's helpful to first establish the "roots" of your taxonomy. In a more traditional, hierarchical taxonomy, there would be only one root. But as you've seen with faceted taxonomy structures, there can be several root terms. Discuss this concept with your SME to see if it makes sense for your organization.

In some cases, a corporate taxonomy structure might be defined for you, even if it hasn't been identified as such. You might have product lines that subdivide into product families that subdivide into product models, etc. If your system will be used to house assets related to those products, it might make sense to mirror that taxonomy rather than reinvent the wheel. Even if it's not an ideal structure, your users are likely to know it. And if they don't know it today, they'll learn it if they stay with the organization for any period of time.

Adherence to a corporate standard taxonomy that was built as a hierarchy doesn't mean you can't take advantage of faceting or other features your system might offer. Consider the following, which depicts a greatly simplified hierarchical taxonomy in combination with facets.

```
Product Family
        ↳ Communications
                ↳ Phones
                        ↳ Intergalactic Mobility®
                        ↳ Globalicious Mobility®
                ↳ Radar
                        ↳ AeroSpyzit Deluxe®
                        ↳ Maritime Motion®
Year
        ↳ 2016
        ↳ 2015
        ↳ 2014
Content Type
        ↳ Advertising
        ↳ Instructional
        ↳ Sales
Formats
        ↳ PDF
        ↳ InDesign
```

The Product Families brand of the taxonomy might come from your corporate standard, but this doesn't preclude you from adding facets that are useful for finding content. In this example, someone could choose a subset of the Product Family branch and then fine-tune results using the added facets below.

Once you have an idea of the scope of terms your SME thinks will be required, take an organizational concept to some users. It doesn't have to be complete—something like what's shown above could work. The idea is to see whether users could see themselves working with the structure. Do they like the faceted approach? Do they have ideas for other facets that you might not have considered?

Also consider the unique requirements of different stakeholders. Your Logistics department might often search for items based on weight or other physical factors that make little or no difference to other groups. When this is the case, consider those requirements. If your system supports granular view permissions on taxonomy nodes, you'll be able to show and hide various nodes and terms based on user groups, which can go a long way toward reducing complexity.

Once you have a sample structure in mind, figure out whether your Sales users know how to find this year's product brochures for, say, the AeroSpyzit Deluxe brand. Would your editors know how to find the layout they need to fix a typo that was reported in the user guide for the Global Mobility brand?

It's much more efficient and effective to talk about taxonomy on paper than it is within a content system. Changes are easier to make, and it helps keep users focused on the topic at hand. When working within a CMS or DAM, users can become distracted to the point where they are unable to differentiate between the taxonomy and user interface elements that might have nothing to do with that taxonomy. Further, in order for a taxonomy to be adequately experienced within a content management system, the content must first be tagged with metadata that would not typically be assigned until the taxonomy was complete. (In the content management world, taxonomy assignments are metadata.)

Inferred Meaning through Hierarchy

By providing a structure of terms that makes sense (a taxonomy), meaning can be inferred from tag assignments that *aren't* specifically made. For example, if "Audi" is found within the Car taxonomy, one can assume that all digital assets tagged with "Audi" are of cars. So when looking for generic car photos, for example, one needn't specifically include "Audi" in the search in order to see those images.

```
Vehicles

    ↳ Cars

        ↳ Audi

        ↳ Lexus

        ↳ Ferrari

        ↳ Jeep
```

The opposite is not true, however. Using the example above, if you were to tag an asset with *Car*, this says nothing about the type of car. So when users search for any of the specific car brand tags, they would not find your content. (This actually depends on the system. Some do offer the option to "search upward" in a hierarchy. But this feature can lead to such confusing results that it's often disabled.)

Diving Too Deep

Benefiting from inferred tag assignments is often the start of a taxonomy strategy discussion that should involve others. For example, should there be another layer of categorization between Cars and each car brand?

Consider the following variation:

```
Vehicles
    ↳ Cars
        ↳ Luxury
            ↳ Audi
            ↳ Lexus
        ↳ Utility
            ↳ Jeep
        ↳ Sport
            ↳ Ferrari
```

While this is no more or less correct that the preceding example, it brings up two important points to consider:

1. Is there a benefit to your organization in having car class (luxury, utility, etc.) inferred in the taxonomy?
2. Does providing this additional layer of granularity create any conflict or confusion?

That second point is worth some serious consideration. For example, top-of-the-line Jeeps can be quite luxurious. Likewise, both Audi and Lexus make all-wheel drive vehicles that rival the utilitarian capabilities of some Jeep models. And if the Audi R8 isn't a luxury sports car, I don't know what is.

While there is no question that Audi, Lexus and Jeep were each Cars, by adding *class* to the hierarchy, you're faced with decisions that can be argued from different perspectives.

When this happens, consider it a Red Flag warning that you might be diving too deeply into taxonomy granularity. This isn't to say that you would always avoid such a situation, but you must consider some important points:

- Increased granularity will require additional user education to make sure everyone is on the same page.
- Increased granularity means you will have to introduce compromises into the definitions of your taxonomy terms in order to account for situations in which the added granularity doesn't perfectly suit a given

situation. For example, "We always classify Jeeps as Utility, regardless of model."

- Increased granularity increases the likelihood of inconsistent tag assignments because there is more human judgment involved.
- Increased granularity requires additional expertise on the part of those adding tags.

A good taxonomy is one that provides a *reasonable* number of options and satisfies a *reasonable* number of situations, all in a way that makes sense to a *high percentage* of users.

In other words, no (complex) taxonomy could be considered perfect. Further, many *good* taxonomies are incomplete. Somewhere between suitable and complete, even the best taxonomies pass from usable to unmanageable.

Consider how long it would take to train someone to use a taxonomy that has only a few terms: Is it a photo of a car, a dog or a chair? Admittedly incomplete and hardly useful, a young child could be trained to categorize photos using this taxonomy. (Assuming all photos were of one of those subjects.)

Once you add levels of granularity, training and judgement requirements increase. Cars, as we've seen, could be subdivided as sports, luxury, utility and more. Dogs could be male or female, let alone size, breed, etc. And chairs could be recliners, bar stools, dining and more. With just this first level of subtopic hierarchy, you've virtually eliminated a young child's ability to accurately categorize your collection.

You won't likely be designing taxonomies for toddlers, but this does illustrate an important point: User knowledge, interest and patience have their limits. There is a "gamification" aspect to tagging content, so long as the task remains easy for the tag editor. Many people derive a sense of organizational satisfaction from adding tags they know will increase the value of the archive. But once those minds are challenged, what could have been a fun game becomes real work and the enthusiasm level drops.

As a goal, you want your taxonomy to be as granular as it needs to be in order to categorize content into meaningful topics that help users find what they need. Anything deeper increases complexity, the likelihood of miscategorization, and the frustration level of your users. Don't subdivide topics forever just because you can. No one will appreciate that.

Derived Controlled Vocabularies

"All taxonomies are controlled vocabularies but not all controlled vocabularies are taxonomies." When I first heard this I had to consider it for a moment. In essence, by creating a taxonomy, you are creating a limited set of terms, even if that set is enormous. By contrast, if a controlled vocabulary is created as a random list of terms, there might be no hierarchical relationship between those terms, thereby eliminating any semantic representation of those terms that we expect from a taxonomy.

That in mind, you might find many situations in which a branch of your greater taxonomy would make for a handy controlled vocabulary. This becomes particularly valuable when you use adaptive metadata schemas that provide granularity on the metadata field level.

For example, say you have the following content classes defined in your adaptive metadata schema:

- Car
- Airplane

When you have a photo of a car, you'd assign the *Car* class. The class, in turn, would provide the following metadata fields:

- Brand
- Model
- Class
- Drivetrain

Your *Airplane* content class might also provide similarly named metadata fields:

- Brand
- Model
- Class
- Propulsion

To make metadata entry fast and more accurate, you'd assign a controlled vocabulary to each field. For Drivetrain, your vocabulary might contain only "Rear-wheel Drive," "Front-wheel Drive," "All-wheel Drive" and "Four-wheel Drive" as options. Propulsion might use only "Propeller" and "Turbine" as vocabulary options.

In the case of the *Brand* fields, you'd assign vocabularies that were lists of brands. The trick would be in isolating the brands that made sense for each content class. For example, Boeing doesn't make cars and Jeep doesn't make airplanes. So it would make no sense to offer those brands as options for the wrong content class.

This is where it makes sense to assign a branch of your greater taxonomy to be used as a controlled vocabulary (CV) for each field.

An example of how that taxonomy might appear follows. Where you see something like `Class:Airplane:Brand`, read this as "the 'Brand' field that is provided by the 'Airplane' class."

```
Airplane
    ↳ Brands (use as CV for Class:Airplane:Brand)
        ↳ Boeing
        ↳ Cessna
    ↳ Models (use as CV for Class:Airplane:Model)
        ↳ 777
        ↳ 172
    ↳ Classes (use as CV for Class:Airplane:Class)
        ↳ Jet
        ↳ Prop
Car
    ↳ Brands (use as CV for Class:Car:Brand)
        ↳ Audi
        ↳ Jeep
    ↳ Models (use as CV for Class:Car:Model)
        ↳ A5
        ↳ Wrangler
    ↳ Classes (assign as CV to Class:Car:Class)
        ↳ Luxury
        ↳ Utility
```

By assigning these taxonomy branches to specific metadata fields (as indicated), you'd provide *content-relevant* controlled vocabulary options for each field. As the taxonomy was updated, those updated values would become part of the vocabularies in use.

As mentioned, CVs can also be nothing more than lists of terms that have no association to other CVs. (Other than being in the same CV.) These are ideal when the terms are generic and would otherwise not fit into your institutional taxonomy.

In addition to the Drivetrain and Propulsion examples used above, you might also see options like:

- Colors
- Camera Angles
- Countries

Term lists like these might fit nowhere in your greater taxonomy, but they are still useful as CVs. If your content system supports linking to external files or resources that can be used as CVs, then you're set. If not, add a Vocabularies branch to your taxonomy tree and put them there, even if they have no relation to anything else in the tree. The net result is the same. (Explore the "view" permissions options for your system to see whether you can hide these random lists from users who view the tree. Doing so, can reduce confusion.)

Tag-test a Sample Collection

As you develop your taxonomy, it's a good idea see how some sample content would fit into that structure before you consider yourself done.

Gather a sample collection of content, maybe 50 pieces that are at least somewhat different from one another. Print out a contact sheet or enter information about each asset into a spreadsheet. The goal is to have a document you can use to enter notes about each piece of content.

Next, print out your proposed taxonomy.

Note on the contact sheet or spreadsheet where you'd classify everything. If a term is missing, make note of that. If the asset would fit equally well into multiple taxonomy locations, make note of that too because it might suggest some redundancy in the tree.

Provide others with blank sheets and ask them to do the same. Make sure you offer no education about the structure—you want to see how far people get without any training.

Once you have a set of completed sheets, compare them. If everyone made the same matches, and there were no missing or ambiguous terms indicated, you're in a good shape. Otherwise, consider the differences. Speak to those users, if necessary, to understand their actions and understandings.

Pay careful attention to any term suggestions. What one user considers as "missing" term might be simply a matter of multiple terms that mean the same thing—synonyms.

Did one user think "airplane" while another thought "jet"? Or did one think "aviation" while another thought "travel"? Determine whether those discrepancies could be managed with synonyms or whether you have a hierarchical conceptual difference that you need to study further. (More on synonyms later.)

If you find that your test users expected certain assets to be located in different parts of the taxonomy, find out why. It might be that users from Marketing think differently about your content than do those in Accounting. If this is the case, you can satisfy both constituencies by creating multiple taxonomies that are restricted to only those groups. (Or you could use the same taxonomy and assign the content to more than one term.)

The problem comes when you have an academic disagreement about the classification of an asset. In other words, User A not only comes up with a different idea than User B, but she can explain why she thinks User B's classification suggestion is wrong. Though most professional content systems will enable you to tag a given asset with as many taxonomy terms as you like, this shouldn't be a means for dispute resolution. If one user's idea is flagged as wrong by a user who makes a compelling case, you'll be reducing the efficacy of your system by trying to make everyone happy.

Metadata Field Considerations

A metadata field *schema* is basically a group of metadata fields you'll use in your content management system. The capabilities inherent in most systems offer you some flexibility with regard to how you design your metadata field schemas. As with taxonomy design, the metadata field options you make available will make a big difference in terms of the value users derive from the system.

Reverse-engineering the Search

When designing a metadata field schema from scratch, it's helpful to think in terms of how users will search for your various types of content. This gives you some guidance with regard to the metadata fields you'll need. For example, people expect to find annual reports based on year, while they expect to find photographs based on objects seen within the photos.

Start by creating a list of the different types of content you'll be managing in your system. A spreadsheet is perfect for this. Try to imagine how users will search for each content type and add your assumptions to the spreadsheet.

This table shows some example content types with three search goals, each of which are intended to represent how users might try to find that content:

Content Type	Search Goal 1	Search Goal 2	Search Goal 3
Stock Photo	keywords	stock agency	usage restrictions
Product Photo	product name	product type	sku

Corporate Reports	year	department	topic
Employee Headshots	employee name	employee ID	title

As the table suggests, when searching for stock photos, users are most likely to start with keywords. Users with more specific needs (and knowledge) with regard to licensing or other business factors, might additionally include an agency name or usage restrictions.

You'll likely be able to imagine many more search goals than three. But, as mentioned, it's important that you focus on the scenarios you expect to address the *majority* of users' goals. In trying to account for all eventualities, you'll build a system so complicated that no one will enjoy using it.

Going through this exercise will provide you with a list of metadata fields you should consider adding to your system. Use the list to determine field type and any other attribute that your system will need to know, as shown below.

Field Name	Field Type	Notes
keywords	controlled vocabulary	List of descriptive tags
stock agency	controlled vocabulary	List of stock vendors
usage restrictions	text	Unstructured field for explanation of any restrictions on use
product name	controlled vocabulary	List of company products
product type	controlled vocabulary	List of company product types or classes

sku	number	Number field that provides enough precision for corporate sku numbers.
year	date	Date field without time option
department	controlled vocabulary	List of company departments
topic	controlled vocabulary	List of company report topics
employee name	controlled vocabulary	List of employees
employee ID	number	Number field that provides enough precision for employee ID numbers.
title	text	Unstructured field for employee titles

The point to this exercise is to have you plan and imagine the field schema on paper before you start building it in the content system. The primary advantages to paper-based schema planning are threefold:

- You can see at a glance your entire metadata field schema, which makes it easier to recognize when something has been forgotten or might be redundant.
- Others who do not have admin access to your system can see the schema and comment, as needed.
- Your planning sheet becomes a specification that provides archival value and enables those actually configuring the system to do so in much less time, and with fewer errors.

No matter how easy it might be to add metadata fields to your system, designing your schemas on paper first is always a good idea. The table above is overly simplified, but your actual spreadsheet will likely contain many more values, such as:

- Localized field labels — What will each field be called in different languages?
- Tooltips — What text will users see when they hover over the field?
- Access limitations — Which user groups should have edit or read-only access to the field?
- Indexing options – Should the field be considered in searches?
- Search ranking – How important is a value match in this field? In other words, when searching for the term "Life on Mars," you might consider matches on the Song Title field to be more important than matches in a Caption field. So, any matches in the Song Title field would appear first in search results.

Determining metadata field attributes like these can be a complex (and confusing) process that requires discussion between several people.

When multiple people are involved in the configuration of a content management system, being able to move tasks outside of the system can be a real time saver for everyone.

For example, your localizer (translator) will be able to work with a spreadsheet much more easily than working in the admin section of the content system. Further, this person might requiring training in the use of your system, which will take time. And you might not want freelancers or casual users to have access to admin sections of the system.

Likewise, the person who writes your tooltips might be from your documentation department. To ensure the tips are properly edited, there might be a complete edit/review workflow that happens using a word processor or other program. Requiring these people to create tips from within a DAM or CMS UI will certainly result in delays, or worse.

Controlling user access to metadata fields isn't typically a field attribute (this is more likely configured in another section of your system), but determining who should be able to see and edit each field is a matter that should be discussed as part of your metadata schema design.

Not all content systems offer all field types. So before you get too deeply into designing the schema, make sure you understand the different field (data) types available to you, and the limitations of each type.

When choosing a controlled vocabulary as a field type, make note of the vocabularies you'll need to have on hand. In some cases, as with the department names example used above, the list will already exist somewhere. In other cases, you'll have to create the vocabulary.

Single vs. Multiple Metadata Field Schemas

Depending on the system you use, you'll either be able to define a single field schema or you'll be able to create and use multiple schemas. The advantage to having multiple different metadata schemas is that you can tailor fit a schema to a given content type.

For example, product shots will likely need metadata values to describe product family, model numbers and perhaps product manager, sales channel and more. None of these values would be of use when managing a press release.

Layering metadata is another advantage to being able to use more than one metadata schema at a time. Your core metadata schema might have all the standard fields you need, while you create additional metadata layers for things like production status, discussion fields and other such metadata values that you don't need or want to be part of the content's metadata forever.

Thinking of metadata schema design in terms of layered "building blocks" of fields makes it easy to assemble more complex per-asset schemas that more precisely suit each piece of content.

Structured Data vs. Unstructured Data

We describe metadata fields that guide or restrict user input as being *structured*. Examples of structured metadata field types include date fields, vocabulary fields and menus (which are essentially controlled vocabularies themselves).

Unstructured data describes fields that permit the user to enter what he or she wants. Text fields are the most common type of unstructured data type found in a content system. But you might also find voice annotations or other data types that permit the user to add virtually whatever information she or he wants.

Vocabularies and taxonomies provide a *structured* approach to metadata. This means there is no wiggle room for users who are tagging assets. For example, if a keyword field permits only certain terms, the user has no choice but to accept one of those standardized terms.

When a system is configured to permit only structured metadata values, several important advantages are realized. Some of those benefits are described in the following sections.

Metadata consistency

Despite one person thinking "car" while another thinks "auto," if each of these synonyms leads to the preferred term, "automobile," the system's metadata remains consistent. Some systems make this possible by showing suggestions to a user editing the metadata. So, when typing "car," the system shows a suggestion for "automobile."

When typing "car," this user sees the system's preferred term, *Automobile*. "Car" can be seen among other synonyms assigned to the preferred term. More on synonyms later.

This also helps those searching for content. When you search for "car," you want to also find content tagged with related terms. It shouldn't be up to the user to play guessing games with the system in order to find what's needed.

Pre-localized values

Structured data values can be localized during system development. This means that the moment an English-speaking user tags a photo with the vocabulary item "Piano," your German-speaking users will see the "Klavier" tag and your Russian-speaking users will see "пианино".

When using unstructured text fields, newly added or edited values must be localized manually. Depending on the size of your system, and the number of additional languages you support, this is a process that can be expensive at best, or forever incomplete, at worst, because new content will always need localization.

Clearer reporting

Metadata *input* consistency comes out on the other side as report clarity. How many "car" images do you have? This is what people are interested in. They don't want to see a different number for each related term, such as "3,200 cars" plus "1,233 autos" plus "935 automobiles."

Reliable data exchange

When moving data between systems, there must be some consistent mapping plan to associate data values. For example, though "automobile" might be the preferred term in *your* DAM or CMS, another system might use "car" as a preferred term. Worse, if the other system isn't using structured metadata, there could be any number of terms used throughout the system.

When you know your data is structured and therefore consistent, mappings become easier to create and manage. It also enables you to anticipate imports of unstructured data so that you can give that data your structure. For example, mapping car, hatchback, sports car and any other such terms to your preferred term "automobile."

Without consistent mappings, a data transfer could end up dropping data or creating superfluous values in the target system. Sticking with the example above, if you have configured your system to use "automobile" as a preferred term, and you import data from a system that uses "car," the term "car" could be added to your taxonomy or vocabularies, making a mess of your diligent attention to structure.

Data validation

Structured data is validated in advance of its use. So spelling mistakes and other typos should (in theory) be eliminated.

Data updates

Over time, some colloquial terms fall out of favor or acquire new meanings. "Chill" was a term 20 years ago that referred to reducing the temperature of something. Today, chill is often used to mean relax. Systems configured to use "chill" as a preferred term for temperature reduction might want to reconsider that use now, due to the word's new meaning in pop culture.

By selecting "refrigerate" or some other term to replace chill's original definition in your structured vocabulary, you instantly update the entire system, reliably. If your system was based on unstructured data, this would be a dangerous search-and-replace operation because instances of "chill" could mean refrigerate or relax, or they might be the noun form of the word.

Structured data not only provides context to users, it provides context to the content system too. When making global data updates, you'll want to be confident that you're not editing the wrong metadata values.

Unstructured data that adds details

Unstructured data refers to freeform text fields into which users can type anything. Captions are good examples. The value of these fields is that they permit the metadata contributor to be expressive and detailed. This is important when the structured fields don't adequately convey what needs to be said about the content.

The downside of unstructured data is that the data is rarely consistent. One user might provide a detailed, factually correct assessment of what's seen in a photo while another might not. Further, reporting on these fields is typically useless. Maybe there's value in knowing when there is or is not a value in the fields, but value-match reporting isn't usually useful. "Field contains apple" is going to find fruit and phones, which probably isn't what you have in mind.

Metadata Field Types

DAM systems are little more than databases. As such, they offer pretty much the same field types as standard databases. The table below shows some examples of common field types and when you might use each type in your metadata schemas.

Field Type	Uses	Structured or unstructured	Notes
Text	Captions, notes, directives, usage restrictions, license terms, etc.	Unstructured, unless a vocabulary has been assigned as an input filter.	Though this is typically the first field type new system designers add, if you believe in the value that a structured approach to metadata provides, text (unstructured) fields should be used only to fill in the blanks that structured fields don't cover.
Number	Costs, statistics, product numbers, etc.	Unstructured, unless an input filter permits only certain values.	Some content systems differentiate between numeric types, such as floating point vs. integer. Being able to specifically choose a numeric data field is most important when calculations will be performed on the field's values, or when the system doesn't sort numbers in text fields as you expect.

Date	Due dates, archive dates, license expirations, etc.	Structured. Even though the concept of "any date" might seem unstructured, the fact that a valid date is required provides some structure.	Date fields enable you to sort based on calendar reference, and they make possible calculations, such as "30 days from now." If your system will span time zones, see what options are available for regional date settings. For example, the system might store a standardized date value that can be adjusted for each connected user's location. The need for this becomes especially important when you consider users working in time zones where it will be "tomorrow" before you've even had breakfast.
Time	Specific times of day, production hours spent, etc.	Structured, for the same reason Date is considered structured.	In some systems, date and time are combined into a single field type. As with date fields, check to see what regional display options you have so that users see time references that make sense to them.

Audio	Voice annotations recorded through mics or imported via audio files.	Unstructured.	The idea of speaking into a computer to add metadata might seem futuristic, but it's really of limited value. This is perhaps the ultimate example of unstructured data that's virtually useless when it comes to searching or sorting results. Where this field type becomes interesting is when the system is used as a kiosk that guest users browse. In these cases, an annotation field could be a "Click here to learn more" audio playback option. But even in this case, it would be better to be able to link to an audio file for playback. This way, you can manage the audio file as you would any other content, complete with its own metadata.

Some content systems offer "Text" and "Controlled Vocabulary" as separate field types. In other systems, a controlled vocabulary field is just a text field with an input filter applied, which is the vocabulary.

If your system is in the latter group, it's important that you (and your system configurators) remember that a vocabulary is to be assigned as an input filter wherever that field is used. Otherwise, when developing alternate interfaces to the system, such as mobile UIs or branded portals, your data could become polluted by uncontrolled input.

Another option you might see is a "rich text" field type. Rich text refers to text that can be formatted (bold, italics, etc.) or embedded with links.

Though rarely found in content systems at the time of this writing (unless they were designed for website content), this feature is a wonderful way to pre-format content that will be displayed on websites or other external resources. Without rich text formatting (or "markdown"), a system can provide only characters in a single font, with no formatting or links.

Worth noting is that some Web browsers will turn what appears to be a valid hyperlink into an actual hyperlink. This can make it appear as though the system is using a rich text field when it isn't.

Some systems might have text field attributes that limit the number of characters permitted in a field. This was a useful consideration back in the day when computers weren't so powerful and memory and hard drive space were scarce. Today, there are few valid reasons for limiting the number of characters that can be entered into a text field. If anything, this would serve only as an annoyance to a user who needed a few more characters to complete his or her thought.

Some systems also differentiate between "single-line" and "multiline" text field types, which can really be confusing at first. As with character limitations, this is more about programmer convenience than it is about user experience. If your system makes this differentiation, make sure you understand why before you start defining your metadata schemas. In most cases, it will be about how the fields are displayed on layouts.

Mandatory Field Values

Web forms are littered with asterisks (*) that indicate which fields must contain values in order for the form to be accepted.

Name ∗

[ ]

E-mail ∗

[ ]

Phone ∗

[ ]

[Let the Spamming Begin]

Mandatory fields on website forms can discourage users from submitting the form. Mandatory fields in a content system can discourage users from added or editing content.

If you're like me, you look at mandatory fields with a sense of resentment and fatigue. Is all this information *really* necessary? Perhaps you don't know the proper value for a field, or maybe there is no good answer for your situation.

My favorite mandatory fields are those "security" questions financial websites force us to endure:

∗ Select one of the following security questions to help us verify your identity:

- *How old were you when you first performed at Carnegie Hall?*
- *What is the middle name of your third great-grandchild?*
- *What was your first pet thinking when it died?*

Worse is when it's clear that the *only* reason a given value is mandatory is that someone wants to sell you something later.

We've all spent time filling out forms at doctors' offices. Family medical history? Dates for all hospital admissions for my entire life? Really? How should I know whether I've ever had a relative with high blood pressure?

Imagine if your exam couldn't begin until the form was absolutely complete. How many phone calls would be you willing to make to hunt down the missing values? How much time would you be willing to spend before you started guessing?

I think about each field for only a few seconds and, if I don't know the answer, I write "N/A," "unknown" or I just leave the field blank. After all, the doctor won't treat my flu symptoms any differently just because she learns that my father's brother was a chain smoker who died from a heart attack.

I know that all this data isn't necessary to treat my immediate needs. Sure, I appreciate the value that a complete medical profile might provide one day. But in the meantime, I have the damned flu and filling out forms isn't making me feel any better.

Fortunately, most medical professionals realize they can treat you without knowing absolutely everything about everything.

Unfortunately, most content system designers don't realize this.

When people design data processing systems, including content management systems, they come up with all sorts of reasons why certain fields should be required:

- The more fields we require, the more complete our data will become.
- The more data we have, the better we will know the user.
- The better we know the user, the better a user experience we can offer that user.
- Certain field values are required in order to process the form request.

The problem with those first three reasons is that they are not at all about users–they are about system managers. Users don't ask for tailored "user experience management." In fact, users want what they want when they want it, and then they want you to leave them the hell alone. They don't want you tracking them across the Web with advertising, and they don't want to see "Welcome Back!" messages when they return to your website.

Does it comfort you to know you're being watched and followed?

For the sake of argument, let's agree that we're decent people who value user privacy and have decided that those first three reasons for mandatory field aren't good enough. This leaves only those fields that are required to process the form request. These are, in my opinion, the only fields that should ever be mandatory.

If you're ever in doubt about which fields should be (ethically) mandatory, ask yourself why you need the data. If you can come up with reasons that directly serve the user's request, then you have reason for making the fields mandatory.

Here are some common web form examples:

- Email – Required if you must email the user a response that cannot (or should not, for business process reasons) be provided in the redirect page that appears after the form is submitted.
- Name – Required if the submission is for a registration or other situation through which the user will be identified by his or her name. (Note that providing a downloaded eBook does *not* require that you know the requester's name.)

Virtually all other fields are debatable:

- Language – If the form is in English, what point is there in asking what language the requester speaks? You can later discover whether the user has a preferred language, assuming your relationship goes deeper.
- Gender – In some languages, proper formal address (Sir or Madame, for example) depends on knowing the person's gender. The problem with this is that it's not clear on the form why gender is being asked, so it just seems intrusive. Further, some people don't self-identify as male or female, so asking them to make a choice between the two is like asking people to choose either "White" or "Black" in a the Race field. Adding instructions to "choose the best option" is not a solution.
- Location – Sales organizations love knowing where someone is so they can route the inquiry to the regional manager, gather stats on regional lead streams and more. They can rationalize this requirement as being one that better serves the requester. In fact, it's all about convenience to the sales and marketing teams. When people ask about your products, they are not asking to speak to your regional account rep or partner. They are simple asking for information they presume can be provided by any number of people, regardless of location.

When designing content system metadata field schemas, these concepts apply equally. The difference is that, in the case of digital asset management, the user is not likely making a request, but adding to the value of the system through new content submissions or metadata editing.

In other words, users don't typically benefit personally from their actions–at least not immediately. This is all the more reason to make new content submissions and metadata editing as painless as possible.

And this means *absolutely no unnecessary mandatory metadata fields*.

Recalling all those medical forms you've had to fill out while your head was pounding and your stomach was turning, think about the state of mind of your users:

- They didn't come to the system for entertainment; they have jobs to do and their time is limited.
- They don't love content management like you love content management; they are there because they are required to be there.
- They don't understand the need for all that metadata like you do.

If the uploading/editing user knows all the values required by your mandatory fields, it might take very little time to provide the metadata. But if mandatory values are unknown to the user, one of two things is going to happen:

1. The user will enter random values (or guesses) just to be able to save the record and move on.
2. The user will cancel the upload or edit.

In the first case, your system becomes polluted with bad metadata. And because bad metadata looks a lot like good metadata, it can be virtually impossible to cleanse the system later. In the second case, you've lost an opportunity to make the system more complete and accurate.

In other words, mandatory metadata fields that were intended to improve the system can yield the exact opposite effect.

Never underestimate the power or disinterest of users. They are in control; not you. Your system will succeed or fail because of user actions, not because of your best intentions.

Still, sometimes you do legitimately require some values. As mentioned, certain values might be required by backend workflows.

For example, if your system is configured to "route" new content to authorized users who will then approve it for general use, you might require uploading users to provide some indication of who would be the best person for that job. Maybe you ask for a department name (via controlled vocabulary) or you ask for general topics (via controlled vocabularies) or some other value (via controlled vocabulary).

Just keep a few things in mind when deciding to make a field mandatory:

1. Choosing an accurate value for the field should never challenge the user. If you ask uploading users to make routing decisions, those decisions should be obvious to everyone.
2. If the user provides misinformation in the field, there should be some way to recognize and correct those values. This could be an audit of all newly uploaded data, or maybe just an audit of the actions of new users.

There you have two simple guidelines for managing mandatory fields. The problem, of course, is that it's not always easy to meet these goals.

When asking for a user's email address or name, you can assume the user will be able to comply with accuracy. (Assuming he or she chooses to do so.) But when asking for routing information or other descriptive values, this might not be so easy.

My recommendation to content system designers is that they provide a means for users to admit when they don't know something. If a user is in a rush to get to lunch, she's more likely to type any random value to a metadata field in order to be able to save the record. She is unlikely to then make a note to herself that she should further investigate the value provided. She's even less likely to ask someone for help.

But if all you ask of her is that she admit uncertainty, you might be surprised at the outcome.

For example, a simple checkbox can be used to flag records that need further attention. Couple this field with a notes field, and you might find users are willing to let you know when questionable metadata has been entered.

If your system supports adaptive metadata schemas, users can add these fields only when needed, which helps keep things clean. These values can later be found by user search or workflow, and verifications can be made before the potentially erroneous data becomes a permanent part of the system.

In providing "honesty" functionality like this, you can reduce the number of mandatory fields to only those absolutely required by automation. In turn, you genuinely provide a better user experience, and you build respect among your user base. They will learn that when the system requires a value, there is good reason.

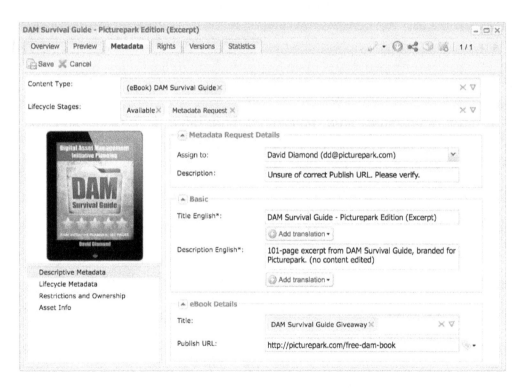

The user has added the *Metadata Request* tag to the Lifecycle Stages field, which adds the Metadata Request Details fields. These fields enable the user to explain the help that is needed and choose to whom the request should be assigned. Once the edit is complete, the Metadata Request tag is removed, which removes the fields it added.

Field Schema Layering

Field schema layering describes having multiple different metadata schemas active on a single piece of content at once, though isolated in layers that make them easier to manage and use.

Consider some (simple) example schemas:

Schema	Field 1	Field 2	Field 3	Field 4
Basic Info	Title	Location	File Format	File Size
License Info	License Holder	Last Renewed	Renewal Due	Contact
Edit Request	Directive	Requester	Due Date	Status
Archive Info	Archive Date	Location	Reason	Contact

The table shows four (simple) metadata schemas: *Basic Info*, *License Info*, *Edit Request* and *Archive Info*. As each schema is added to a piece of content, the fields provided by that schema become available on the content record. Content that has not been assigned a given schema would not have the metadata fields the schema provides.

What's interesting about the metadata fields provided by each schema shown is that they would never all be needed at once. For example, you wouldn't have an open edit request on content that has been archived. What's more, some of these fields would never be required for some content. Content created in house, for example, wouldn't likely need licensing info. And there would certainly be no point in having archive info metadata fields show up on content that has not been archived.

Content management systems (being based on legacy database technology) have traditionally required that all metadata fields that might ever be used throughout the content lifecycle be included in the base metadata schema, visible at all times to users.

If all these metadata fields were added to a single schema, this is what users would see when opening a content record:

Schema (Basic Info)
License Holder
Directive
Archive Date
Location
Last Renewed
Requester
Location
File Format
Renewal Due
Due Date
Reason
File Size
Contact
Status
Contact

Keeping in mind that this is an overly simplified example of schemas, you can see how things can become complicated. First off, without the context of the schema name itself, the field labels would have to be more descriptive. Otherwise, users would see two Location and Contact fields, without any indication of which was which. The Reason, Requester and Archive Date fields would be confusing, offering no hint about their respective purposes.

To remedy the confusion, systems might offer labels that can be used to separate the fields into groups. This is a giant step forward with regard to usability, but it doesn't satisfy the most important question with regard to making the system easier to use: *Why use metadata fields that are not required or make no sense?*

The point to metadata field layering is that users add only the fields that are needed, and only when and while they're needed. More importantly, they can add a set of fields based on adding a tag that's easy to understand.

The following table includes some content examples, and shows how each metadata schema listed above might be applied during the first five years of the content's lifecycle:

Content Type	Newly Created or Acquired	One Year Old	Five Years Old
Stock Photo	Basic License Info	Basic License Info	Basic License Info
Employee Photo	Basic	Basic Edit Request	Basic Archive
Annual Report	Basic	Basic Archive	Basic Archive
Brochure	Basic	Basic Edit Request	Basic Edit Request

During the lifecycle of a given piece of content, the metadata fields needed to manage that content will likely change. This is why single-schema systems can be so cumbersome: You're managing newly acquired content right alongside content that's years old. The metadata needs of aging content differs just as the metadata needs of different content types differs.

In the example of the stock photo, you'd need Basic and Licensing Info metadata fields immediately and indefinitely. You might, at some point, archive that asset. If so, you'd just add the Archive metadata schema.

After a year, an employee photo might need an edit to account for some cosmetic change, such as an increase in grey hair that comes from a year's worth of working in a system that has too many mandatory fields. If that employee leaves at five years, the photo would be archived. (And the mandatory metadata fields could be the blame.)

The active lifespan of an annual report is a year, so that's when it would make sense to add the Archive schema. You might also consider a single annual report file to be updated each year, in which case you might use the Edit Request schema. But most organizations would want to keep each report as a separate asset, for archival reasons.

The "Summer Products" brochure would be updated each year. The Edit Request schema is perfect for this purpose. Once the updates for a given season were done, the "Edit" schema could be removed. It could be added back again later, as needed.

By organizing metadata fields into layers that can be easily added and removed by users, each piece of content in your system can have an ever-changing metadata schema that's always relevant for the current status of that content.

Here are a few more metadata schema layer ideas you might find useful:

Schema	Field 1	Field 2	Field 3	Field 4
Distribution Approval	Art Director Signature	Art Director Signed Date	Editor Signature	Editor Signed Date
Campaign Content	Campaign Name	Regions	Date Range	Contact
Webinar	Recording Date	Host	Guests	Recording URL
White Paper	Page Count	Language	Related Product	Author

One of the main advantages of layering metadata fields is that it enables you to become quite specific with regard to the information you manage in your system. If you were forced to provide all these fields across all content all the time, you'd be far more likely to pare down the information you track into only the most basic metadata values.

When you start to think about your metadata schema design, you'll likely realize that thinking in terms of different schema building blocks not only makes sense, it's most likely how you think about metadata right now anyway.

In summary, metadata schema layers offer the following advantages over using a single schema across the entire system:

- Metadata fields are added only if needed, which helps keep the system easier to manage and use.
- Metadata fields can be added or removed as required, to suit the content's current state.
- Metadata fields can be granularly specific, so that you can track all the info you need to track, without making a mess of the system by adding scores of irrelevant metadata fields to every piece of content.
- Users aren't confused or otherwise slowed by having to consider a number of fields that make no sense.
- Metadata values are (likely) more accurate and relevant because users aren't confused about a field's intended purpose.
- Field-level permissions are easier to configure because you can think of fields in groups and purpose. For example, only certain users might be authorized to add or remove the Distribution Approval schema, while the fields it contains would be editable only to the art director and editor, as you would expect.
- Metadata field sets can be isolated by intended audience, such as fields used for internal production versus those used for publication or exchange with other systems.

That last point is important for organizations that must employ one or more metadata standards in their content management system, yet they want to also be able to add and use metadata fields that are of value only for internal purposes.

Adopting a Metadata Standard

A metadata standard is a group of metadata values defined by or recognized by some authority organization to collectively satisfy a certain information management requirement.

For example, a metadata standard used for the management of automobile information might include:

- Manufacturer
- Model
- Year
- Color
- VIN

As simple and obvious as this schema seems, the value it provides is that it would be a *standard*, meaning that all who adopted it would be managing compatible metadata. So if you needed to get automobile metadata from your system to, say, an insurance system that also supported the standard, you'd know what fields would be expected, and in what formats.

Without a standardization of schema, any transfer of metadata between systems would be an arduous task of auditing the schemas of both systems and then building a mapping table that could reliably move the data between the systems. (And then hoping nothing changes on either end with regard to the metadata schemas in use.)

But even when data transfer isn't a goal, a metadata standard helps organizations consider all the information they need to track for a certain type of content.

A nice example of an early metadata standard comes from the International Press Telecommunications Council (IPTC). The IPTC standard was originally developed to enable news agencies to share photos with some assurances that all required metadata would be available. As such, it includes metadata fields, such as Caption, City, Event, Photographer and Urgency–all fields you would expect news agencies to care about.

The Wikipedia page for Metadata Standards includes a list of standards, but this list is a mere fraction of all those available. In fact, there is no complete list of metadata standards because the scope of each standard varies so much.

For example, standards like IPTC Core, Dublin Core and EXIF are in wide use across many different applications, so they are virtually always part of any discussion on metadata standards. But individual industries (and even companies within those industries) have developed metadata standards of their own. The Publishing industry has a standard called ONIX that's used for the sale of online books, while the XBRL standard is in use across financial applications. There are many more such standards.

The decision to adopt a standard often requires some discussion. For some, the adoption of a standard is a no-brainer, while others question the value in adhering to some limited schema that might not perfectly represent the organization's needs for metadata management.

Below are some reasons why adopting a standard might be a good idea:

- There is a defined and successful standard in use for your industry (or company)
- You need to exchange data with other systems that use a standard
- It's important that you track specific metadata for compliance or other reasons
- You have found a standard that closely reflects the metadata you need to track
- You want to have certain metadata field values embedded into files that are distributed from your system (more on that later)

Layering metadata standards

If your content system enables you to layer metadata schemas, you can support whatever standard you need, while also tracking additional metadata values that might be useful only for internal discussions. Because metadata layering keeps fields separate, there is no danger in "polluting" an adopted standard through the addition of custom schema layers.

If your system doesn't support adaptive or layered metadata schemas, you'll need to make sure it's clear which fields are part of any standard you adopt. You might be able to do this through field labeling of the nonstandard fields, if it doesn't become too cumbersome.

You'll also need to make sure that none of the nonstandard metadata is exported or otherwise made available to other systems that expect you to provide metadata in the format of the approved standard.

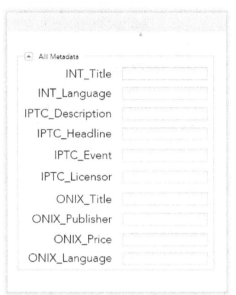

Content systems that support metadata schema layering (left) enable you to add tags to get the fields you need. Because the fields for each standard are managed in layers, they remain discrete, regardless of their names. When using content systems that don't support layered metadata (right), you'll need to name each field to make clear to users to which standard the field belongs. (Note there are "Internal" and "ONIX" fields for *Title* and *Language*.)

An additional benefit to being able to layer your metadata standard fields is that it makes it easier for you to determine which user groups should have access to the fields. Using the image above as an example, you might want all users to have access to your internal metadata fields, while IPTC fields are accessible only to editors, and ONIX fields are available only to those who manage your book sales.

Standards as a starting point for discussion

If you expect (or know) that you'll never need to exchange standardized metadata with other systems, and you have no audit or other reason to ensure compliance with a given metadata standard, you might still want to adopt an established standard as a starting place for your own schemas.

In fact, when starting internal discussions about which metadata values you will need to track, presenting a metadata standard can be a great way to get the discussion going. When those unfamiliar with metadata see the fields listed in a standard, it can help them gain a better understanding of exactly what we mean by metadata. That, in turn, can make the conversation more efficient and meaningful.

If you work in an industry for which you can find no established metadata standard, you might consider joining forces with others to create a standard.

If you work for a large, multi-division organization, start by contacting your counterparts in other divisions. Discuss your common needs and see if you can come up with something that makes sense for all considered.

For example, a medical institution might have metadata concerns that span departments, such as:

- Is the content affected by any governmental privacy regulations?
- Is the content related to patient care?

Once you have what you consider to be a viable standard for your organization, consider proposing it to others in your industry. Conferences and conventions can be good avenues to present such things. But you might also promote the proposal through public discussion groups, such as those on LinkedIn, or through industry trade publications.

There's no need to go through an organization like the ISO in order to get your standard officially recognized. In fact, a good dose of marketing and promotion will likely be more effective at spreading the word to those who need to know.

When reading content management software brochures and websites, you'll hear about the metadata standards each systems support. In fact, any system that enables you to create custom metadata fields without limitation can be configured to support virtually any metadata standard, including any you develop in house.

Keep in mind, metadata is not just used by CMS and DAM systems. Product information management (PIM) systems and other business applications also have a need for metadata. When a standard is in use, it's easier to move metadata between these systems.

In summary, standardize on *something*. As you get deeper into the evolution of your content management initiative, you'll see how being able to rely on a consistent set of metadata fields makes many things much easier.

Embedding Metadata into Distributed Files

The Extensible Metadata Platform (XMP) is a technology that enables applications to embed (write) certain metadata values into files, and to read values that are embedded into files. The value of XMP is that important metadata values, such as copyright or usage restrictions, can travel along with your files, no matter where the files go. This enables the handlers of those files to learn of and comply with your terms of use.

Higher end DAM and content management systems enable system configurers to determine which metadata fields should be written back to files. This matters because you don't likely want all your metadata written back into your files.

Files that have no embedded metadata can become "orphaned," with no direct connection to your organization. Handlers of those files who want to comply with any directives within the files find no such directives and therefore have no idea how the content can and cannot be used.

File names are sometimes used to identify content owners, but file names are too easily changed by handling users. Though it's also possible for handlers to change embedded metadata values, doing so takes a bit more effort, so it's not likely something that will happen as innocently as a file name change.

An additional concern for content owners who decide to embed important metadata values is that some social media networks strip that embedded metadata when files are posted. So, despite your best efforts to claim ownership and usage directives, that data can be removed without your permission. If stripped files are then distributed further, your embedded metadata is lost.

The IPTC works with concerned members of the metadata community to keep tabs on which social media websites are offenders. The Embedded

Metadata Manifesto website is where those findings are published and updated.

If embedded metadata is important to you, you might want to instruct your marketing teams and employees in general to avoid posting your images to social media websites that strip this data. The problem is that some of the world's most popular social media networks are the worst offenders.

"The Copyright Killings" webinar, recorded in 2013, features IPTC managing director, Michael Steidl, PLUS Coalition president, Jeff Sedlik, and metadata advocate, David Riecks speaking about this topic. You can view the webinar at: http://ck.ContentManagementBook.com

At the bottom of the webinar page is a list of useful resources for those interested in embedded metadata, and furthering the cause of the Embedded Metadata Manifesto.

Define Some Policy

There's good reason for a section on content management policy to be included in a book about metadata:

- Metadata design should support and reflect policy, and
- Metadata design should enable users to more easily adhere to policy, whether or not they're aware of the policy

If you'd like to avoid "the tail wagging the dog," it's a good idea to have some policies in place (or at least in mind) *before* you draft your metadata schemas and taxonomy structures. In fact, designing metadata and taxonomy in adherence to policy is much easier because it gives you clear goals and it makes decision making easier:

- Question: Should we configure the system to permit people to download without logging in?
- Answer: What does the policy on downloads say?

When you consider the hundreds and hundreds of decisions that will need to be made throughout the design and configuration of your content management system or DAM, and when consider that the people working on the system architecture might not be able to read your mind, it becomes clear how much time can be saved by having a clear policy document that can be used to guide development.

Here are some other key advantages of considering policy before designing metadata:

- Policy provides you with the "what are we trying to do?" framework, which is essential to keep in mind when designing metadata, taxonomy and the rest of the system.

- When obtaining signoff for schemas and taxonomies, it's helpful to be able to point to policy as the driving force behind your decisions. This can help you navigate through what could be an ocean of opinions about how things should be done or what's important.
- If a limitation inherent in a system you own or are considering prevents you from being able to adequately adhere to a given policy, you can reconsider the purchase or, if the system has already been purchased, you'll know in advance what limitations you'll have. (Which will likely result in a modification to your policies.)

Content management policy can also be used as a checklist of sorts to help you estimate how much more work needs to be done before the system can be launched, and it helps you better decide when you're ready for launch. For example, if all your most important policies have been accounted for, maybe you're ready for a soft launch.

What Content Management Policy Looks Like

After reading the start of this section, you no doubt now feel like a kid on Christmas morning who has been told to read all the instruction manuals and search online for safety advisories and recall notices before playing with any of your new toys.

If this is you, you're not alone. The authoring, approval, implementation and enforcement of policy can be such a downer for system managers that they avoid it entirely, often to the peril of their systems.

Here are some popular excuses people offer to explain their avoidance of the creation of content management policy:

1. We don't have time to define policy because we need to get the system up and running.
2. Our requirements are simple, so we don't need content management policy.
3. Policy is boring.

Most new content managers agree with all three of these points–especially the third. Worse, system vendors won't typically press the issue because few customers are willing to pay a vendor to help them define policy. (As if most vendor employees would even know how to go about defining policy.)

The problem is that policy has a bad reputation it doesn't necessarily deserve.

Content policy doesn't have to be a hundred-page document structured in some academic format that was taught in school on the day you went skiing. Content policy can be as simple as a few sentences. In most cases, of course, you'll want to get more detailed than this; but there's no reason you can't start out with just the broad stroke points that matter most. You can fill in the details later.

Ironically, a stumbling block for some getting started with a policy document that governs taxonomy is the taxonomy of the document: How do you organize content policy?

Personally, I take a content-focused approach to all things content-related. Though you might have different departments, target markets, partner channels, products and other considerations that *seem* related to your system, at the core of all of it is your content.

A secondary benefit of a content-focused approach to policy definition is that you'll likely find it is the different content types you manage that most closely define the boundaries of the permissions and policies you'll need.

For example, if I were to ask you what policies should govern your Marketing department's use of your content, you might struggle to find a starting point of discussion. But I were to ask you what policies should govern access to your strategic documents, you'd likely be able to start speaking immediately:

- They should be seen only by a limited number of people
- They should be marked "confidential"
- They should be approved by certain people before anyone sees them
- They should be dated and versioned

Before reading on, take a few moments to consider the policies you already have that govern your content, some of which might not even be officially documented:

- Press releases — How are they managed?
- Product info — When does it become available?
- Budgets — How far in advance of the start of a fiscal year do these discussions begin?

Even if you don't personally know how your press releases are managed, chances are you can find someone who does.

Here's a basic policy structure you can use for each content type you expect to manage:

- What defines a piece of content as being of a certain content type? In other words, what makes a strategic document a strategic document? How does a press release differ from a blog post? When does a technical document become suitable for promotional use?
- What metadata do you need to track for each content type? For example, "Employee Headshot" content might require an employee's name, start date, status of employment, etc.
- What *fixed* access rules affect the content type? "Fixed" refers to permissions that won't change throughout the lifecycle of the content. Maybe the Finance department should always have access to budget documents, regardless of their state. Maybe editors should always have access to press releases. Maybe a small team of senior managers should always have access to everything.
- What *dynamic* access rules affect the content type? Here is where you define permissions that are rules-based. For example, "press releases are available to the public only after they have been approved by an editor and a manager, and their embargo dates have expired."
- How are revisions and corrections handled for this content type? If someone finds an error in an annual report, what's the process for reporting that error? Should the document be updated or, for legal reasons, should the document remain as is, with the error noted in an addendum?
- What circumstances define when content should be taken offline and optionally archived? For example, if an error is found in an annual report, should the report be taken offline while the error is examined? If

so, do you add placeholder content to explain to people what's going on? Do you do this via metadata instead? Should product information for an end-of-life product remain online? Should it be marked "Legacy Product" and left alone, or should it be taken offline and archived? By contrast, maybe press releases are never taken offline because of the historical value they provide.

The benefits of having these questions answered for each type of content you'll manage include:

- There is no confusion over what happens during each state of the content's lifecycle. If there is still confusion, your policy is confusing or incomplete, or you need to educate your users.
- You have a "map" you can use to confirm compliance across your content collections. For example, have any press releases gone out without a manager's approval? If so, you can conduct an investigation to see what went wrong.
- You have a standard with regard to how things are typically handled, which can be helpful in the event legal action is ever brought against your organization. For example, if an analyst misuses some piece of information that was published from your system under embargo, and you can show that the analyst was aware of your policy and that you made all reasonable efforts to properly secure the content, you might have a case that would otherwise be difficult to defend if your only defense was, "He should have known to not release that until June."
- You have a roadmap of the metadata schemas, permissions and automated workflows you'll need in your system.

That last point provides you with the most immediate benefit as a metadata/taxonomy designer. The policy template questions posed above are not much different than questions you'd need to have answered anyway. What I'm recommending is that when you find those answers, you make them the start of a policy document that becomes official. Otherwise, that institutional knowledge will live only in your brain. Others who work with the system after you might have no idea why something was configured a certain way, which could lead to configuration changes that could jeopardize the system's ability to help users adhere to policy.

Adapting Existing Policy

Your organization might not have content-specific policies in place–especially if you've never before used a DAM or content management system. But there might be some "understood" policies in place that govern the traditional management and movement of your content.

The following can help you get your content policy document started:

- Identify the person in charge of each content type and identify another person who can be considered a user of that content. (The user should be different than the person in charge.)
- Interview these people about how things work for their respective content types. Ideally, both individuals will explain the same process and requirements. If you hear different stories from each, ask the person in charge for clarification and explain that at least one user isn't aware of the way things should work. (Better to get this resolved before you configure policy errors into the system.)
- Use what you learn to draft your content policy for each content type. Once you have a fairly complete document, run it by your content authorities for buy-in and approval, and run it by your user contacts to get their perspectives.

It might be best to ask your chosen content authorities how things work rather than ask if they have drafted official policy documents. If there is such a document, you'll likely be pointed to it. If there is no such document, there's no use in shaming the person into deciding one is suddenly needed. The last thing you want to hear is, "Let me draft a policy document and get it approved. Once that's done, I'll get back to you." You'll be waiting forever.

Take an active role in these interviews–question the information you get until you're absolutely certain you understand all steps involved. People who know a process/policy *too well* can sometimes omit details they take for granted. When it comes to translating policy to system functionality, all process steps must be detailed.

Make sure to ask what happens when things don't go according to plan. For example, if you learn that licensed images are reviewed and optionally renewed 30 days before license expiration, ask what happens when the reviewer or person who handles licensing isn't available. If there are no others who have the authority, time and ability to accomplish these tasks, you might want to shift that policy to take effect 90 days before license expiration.

As a backup measure, maybe create and use a general email address that reaches multiple people so that you know license notifications will reach at least one person. This is also a handy way of avoiding have to update content system configurations when employees come and go.

The goal is not watertight system configuration that can effectively handle all situations–that won't be possible in many situations, or it will take too much effort to realize. Instead, you want to make sure that what can be easily managed by the system is managed by the system, and what requires human interaction can be handed off with minimal process interruption, and with absolutely no process breakdown.

If you're thinking this sounds like business process management, that's because it is. *Content management* without *business process management* is called *file management*. And all file management requires is a clever filename and folder structure.

Processes that are fairly complex can be illustrated as flow charts in various software programs. This is a useful exercise if you want to establish some record of sign-off with regard to each process. It's not a trivial expense to have automated content management workflows built, so you could waste thousands in services expenditures if you're building flows that are wrong.

If a process makes sense, you'll find that it's pretty easy to structure as a flow chart, even if you're not personally familiar with the process itself. You'll also find it's easier (and less costly) to implement flows in content systems when they make sense.

If a process makes no sense to you, it won't make sense to your system either. It's not that business process designers are (necessarily) stupid, but when consensus is the goal, compromise can be the outcome. What was started out as solid policy might have devolved into a hack that satisfied too many people. If this is the case, you have two choices:

1. Configure the system to reflect the bad policy or process, or
2. Discuss your concerns with the people in charge and try to get the policy changed

Not to drive the child-on-Christmas-morning in you into a full frustration melt down, but the second option is the correct answer here.

Humans instinctively get around bad policy by making on-the-fly decisions and exceptions, when needed. For example, if press release policy dictates that press releases require the approval of a manager, and the only available manager is on vacation, a human can manually verify that a release is ready to go, just by making some phone calls or sending some emails. But an automated workflow doesn't know how to reason like this, let alone how to use a phone. (Though, granted, it's becoming increasingly difficult to find people willing to use phones for phone calls.) For this reason, a policy that doesn't account for what to do in the event that a required manager isn't available should be considered bad policy that will eventually delay things.

Policy Reviews and Revisions

Policy that works well is often invisible–once we know the rules, we don't think about them much. When you approach a traffic light that's red, you know to stop your car; when the light turns green, you know to go. This is traffic policy managed through a technological interface that's easy to understand and consistent in execution, both of which are important considerations.

By contrast, imagine if each town used different colors for stop and go. You cross a border and see blue and orange lights. Not such a big deal; right? You find out what the new colors mean and you adapt.

Maybe another town uses the red and green lights you know, but they flash those colors to convey even more information. Say, for example, that flashing red means "slow down for a stop," while solid red means "stop" while flashing green means "get ready to go" while solid green means "go."

City planners could argue that this is a cost savings per traffic light of one third because they don't need that third light for yellow. It's difficult to argue with this logic until you consider some of the potential pitfalls of this seemingly more efficient policy:

- A light might be interpreted as flashing when it's about to burn out
- Ambient lighting conditions could make it difficult to determine whether a light is flashing
- A light that's switching between solid colors could be perceived as flashing
- Motorists need to be able to ascertain a traffic light indicate in an instant, rather than having to wait to see if it's going to stay on or flash
- What indication should be used when the traffic light is known to be nonfunctioning?

So, while this two-light paradigm might save a city money, it might result in motorist confusion and, in turn, an increase in collisions.

If you think confusing lighting policy doesn't exist, you can see here (http://faa.ContentManagementBook.com) what the United States Federal Aviation Administration expects pilots to remember.

I once had a flight instructor ask me if I knew what to do in the event that my aircraft radios went dead, requiring me to land based on light signals from the tower. I responded, "Push the yoke all the way forward, apply full power, and close my eyes until I felt the impact and heard the boom."

She responded, "I know, right?"

The lesson here is that policy efficiency doesn't always align with user experience, tolerance or mental capacity. It's one thing to expect pilots to remember that ridiculous light policy when they're on the ground; it's quite another to expect a pilot to remember this when a radio has failed in flight.

The same holds true for content users, though their "emergencies" are likely less dramatic. Still, when someone is on deadline and someone else is breathing down his or her neck for a document, adherence to policy can quickly become a lesser priority.

Respect for policy adherence isn't that much greater even under perfect situations. Policy that is too cumbersome will be ignored or overridden, no matter what threats you make to your workforce, or how many freshly baked cookies you bring into the office. Do you always drive the posted speed limit when it makes no sense to you to do so?

Though we admire rebellious human spirits, we admire them less when rebellion leads to the mishandling of our content. For this reason, it's best to consider policy a "living" document for which you are always willing to receive input and make warranted changes.

Make sure users know where to go to learn about policy and how to report policy they think isn't working. Your system might offer some contact functions that can help in this regard. If not, create an easy-to-remember email address or other contact option and encourage people to use it.

Once per quarter or year (or whatever interval makes sense for you based on the input you receive), review your policies. In fact, as soon as a policy is put into place, schedule a reminder on your calendar to review it.

By considering user challenges to each policy, you gain three things:

1. You can make smart policy changes where possible
2. You can educate users about why a difficult policy exists and why it cannot be changed
3. You know where users are most likely to ignore policy

That third consideration is important because it enables you to adjust your system configuration to expect violations. For example, if an unpopular policy states that "manager approval is required when sharing strategy documents from the system," you might want to add an option when strategy assets are shared that asks the user to provide the name of the approving manager.

Users are less likely to lie about getting an approval than they are to "forget" to get the approval. This increased accountability might be all that's required to secure the compliance you need.

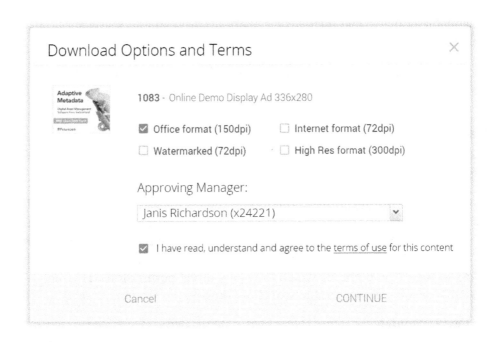

By requiring users to indicate they have read usage policy, and under whose authority they download the content, you help ensure your content will be used in accordance with policy, even after it leaves the system.

Policy Example Questions

Consider these two goals when creating your content management policy:

1. Ensure the organization's requirements are met
2. Account for situations in which user confusion will adversely affect productivity

Remember that content policy shouldn't only involve content inside the DAM or content management system. Your system is just one place your content will exist over its lifetime. While it's true that you won't have total control over content that leaves your system, you still have some influence over employees, partners and customers who use your content outside that system.

Keeping in mind that a policy violation can often been innocent in nature, the first step in the avoidance of such situations is to make clear, fair, reasonable policies, and then ensure everyone who should know about them does know about them.

Below are some user-perspective questions designed to be the basis for policy that can guide those users.

Section: Use of Content

User Goal: I want to use a piece of content that's in the system, but the system won't let me access it.

Technology Solution: Ensure you have a means for users to make requests, be they from within the system, via email or some other means. Make sure it's easy for users to make such requests, and make sure someone responds to the requests. Some content management systems have features that enable users to request content for which they lack direct permissions. If yours doesn't, develop a comparable workflow outside the system.

Policy Example:

Access to Unauthorized Content

Users who want to use content that is not directly available to them, should email policy@YourBusinessOrg.com for approval.

Email requests should contain:

- *The unique identifier of the content. This can be seen at the bottom of the Content Details window. This number is required because it's the only unique value available to identify the specific content.*
- *The intended use case for the content. Briefly describe how the content will be used. This helps the responsible person determine whether the content should be released to the requesting user. It also helps ensure approval in the shortest time possible, because follow-up emails will not be required.*

Requesting users will receive a response within 2 hours. If a response is not received in that time, the requesting user should:

1. *Call the Policy department at x1312. Have the unique identifier of the requested content on hand. The Policy department will approve the*

request immediately or provide a time at which the approval will be granted or denied. It is incumbent upon the Policy department to communicate back to the requesting user.

2. *If the Policy department is unreachable or fails to respond to the requesting user in accordance with this policy, the requesting user should report this to his or her supervisor. That supervisor should then contact the Director of Policy Control at x1534.*

This example addresses important considerations for this and other policies:

- Business process — How does the process work?
- Accountability — Who is responsible for each step?
- Measurability — How does the requesting user know when it's time to escalate a request?

Things could go even deeper: What happens if the requesting user's supervisor is on holiday or forgets to follow up? What happens if the Director of Policy Control isn't available or doesn't respond?

You have to decide for your organization (and for each policy) how deep and granular you need each policy to be. Similar to the discussion about taxonomy granularity, policy that tries to account for all possibilities could be virtually impossible to understand.

In the interest of creating a placeholder document that can be later sussed out with the details you need, the above could be written like this:

Access to Unauthorized Content

1. *Email policy@YourBusinessOrg.com. Include the asset ID number.*
2. *If no response, call x1312.*
3. *If still no response, ask supervisor to follow up.*

Though these brief bullet points don't answer all questions, they do provide a starting point for discussion and decision at a later point in time.

Section: Tagging

User Goal: I need to know which tags to assign to new content.

Technology Solution: If your system is configured to permit only certain users to tag or otherwise edit assets (which is common), in order to make this policy possible, your permissions schema must be configured to:

- Enable edit-access to new content for your editors (remember, this particular policy is about newly added content, not existing content)
- Enable read-access to the tags editors will need
- Enable edit-access to the tags structure, if (other) policy permits new to be created on-demand

Policy Example:

Tagging New Content

Content newly added to the system is accessible only to users in the Content Check-in *group. Any member of this group (editor) may accept and work on newly added content.*

The process of checking in newly added content is:

1. *The editor opens the new content and selects her or his name from the "Check-in Editor" drop down menu. If the editor's name is not found within the menu, he or she must close the content without making changes, and notify DAMAdmin@YourBusinessOrg.com that his or her name is missing from the Check-in Editors menu.*
2. *The editor must choose one or more content classes that best describe the content. Content classes available within the system are defined <u>here</u>. Editors are discouraged from adding more than two classes per content, but the final choice of classes is up to the editor.*
3. *Depending on the content class(es) chosen, the metadata field panel will be augmented with additional fields. The requirements for each field are defined in the content class definition. A list of all available content classes is <u>here</u>. Editors shall familiarize themselves with each content class, its purpose and its requirements.*
4. *Once all fields include values that are in accordance with the policies set forth by the content class, the editor may save and close the record.*

If the editor:

- *Does not know the proper value to be entered into a metadata field, or*
- *Cannot find at least one suitable content class,*
- *Thinks of a content class that best suits the content but is not available,*

she or he must select the Metadata Incomplete *checkbox, and enter a note into the Reason text field that appears near the check box. This note will be automatically forwarded to the system's schema editor. No further action on the part of the editor is required.*

Section: Archived Content

User Goal: I need to know when content becomes suitable for archiving.

Technology Solution: The system must have some means for differentiating between active and archived content. If required by policy, the system must be able to move content marked as "archived" to a different storage location. Search indexes might need to be updated to exclude archived content, if required by policy. If required, the system must provide a means for reactivating archived content and, if necessary, moving that content back to active storage.

Policy Example:

Archived Content

Content is archived in accordance with policy set forth in the <u>content classes</u> used to define the content. Where two or more classes provide differing rules for when content should be archived, the content shall be archived in accordance with the class that offers the longest active lifecycle.

Regardless of assigned class, content may archived by an authorized editor before the end of its active lifecycle under the following circumstances.

- *The content is deemed no longer useful.*
- *The content is part of a collection that has been determined to offer no further use to the organization.*
- *The content is part of a collection that, for licensing or other legal reasons or concerns, has been determined to be off-limits to users.*

- *The content was used for the production of derivative content, and offers no further value on its own.*

An authorized editor, as defined for this purpose, describes a user who is a member of the Editors and Archivists groups. No other user is authorized to archive content, even if that user's group associations permit the action of archiving content.

Authorized editors are permitted to return any piece of content to active use at any time, providing the following conditions are satisfied:

- *There are no laws, contracts, licenses, rules or other restrictions that would prevent the content from being lawfully used, in accordance with all organizational policies.*
- *There are no known political, cultural or other sensitivities that would result in controversy surrounding the intended use of the asset. For example, an archived photograph of Adolph Hitler might be considered acceptable when used in conjunction with a historical piece. Such a photo may not be used to promote a current political ideal, draw a comparison or contrast with modern day persons, or any other use that would be deemed inflammatory.*

When bringing archived content back to active service, the authorized editor becomes the Responsible Person of the asset. (This is set automatically by the system.) The editor must therefore agree to be contacted by others regarding the content, and further agree to follow-up with user inquiries in accordance with the obligations of a content object's Responsible Person, as defined elsewhere.

Additional Policy Considerations

The few policy examples offered above might spark additional ideas as to what sorts of considerations should be covered under a more complete content policy document.

Below are some additional ideas. You'll see when reading through this section that there is virtually always a tight connection between the rules and the supporting technology. The technology must make the rules possible, without undue hardship or inconvenience to users. This is main reason I encourage organizations to think about content policy before they start shopping for DAM or content management software.

System Considerations

- Who owns the content management system?
- How often is the system re-evaluated for continued efficacy?
- Are user-satisfaction surveys sent at regular intervals? If so, how are responses handled?
- Who has purchase authority on behalf of the system?
- What is the reporting/response plan for when the system is offline?
- How is content added to the system backed up?
- What is the process for restoring content when it's determined that live content has been lost?
- Who has the authority to order a content restoration from backup?
- Are backups tested periodically to ensure integrity?

Adding Content

- Who can add new content? Are anonymous uploads permitted or must each uploading user be logged in?
- Who should be notified when new content is added? How will those notifications be handled?
- From where should content contributors be able to add content? (Mobile, desktop, ftp, etc.)
- Are any embedded metadata values required in content added to the system?
- Do you accept content in all file formats?
- Are there any file size restrictions on the content you'll accept?
- Will content contributors be required to accept terms before starting an upload?
- Are there quotas on the amount of content each individual can upload?
- How do you handle duplicate content?
- How do you handle uploaded content that is later determined to be in violation of copyright? Do you just remove it, or do you also inform and educate the uploading user?
- Should someone be designated the "owner" of the content?

Editing Content

- Who can edit content?
- Should notifications be sent about content edits? If so, to whom?
- Should policy define what's added to unstructured (text) fields, such as captions?
- What necessitates a content edit?
- How soon after content is editing in one language must it be localized to other supported languages?
- What is the process for having content edits localized?
- Is there a review process to assure accuracy on newly edited or localized content?

Deleting Content

- Who can delete content?
- Will deleting users be required to explain why they're deleting content?
- Under what circumstances may content be deleted?
- Should notifications be sent about deleted content? If so, to whom?
- Will there be a waiting period for the permanent deletion of content? For example, once deleted, should the system keep it available for x days before it is purged, as a safety precaution?
- Who should have access to the deletion logs?

Editing Taxonomies

- Who can add new terms?
- Under what circumstances may a new term be added?
- Should terms be singular or plural? Examples: Car or Cars; Ox or Oxen
- Is there a discussion/approval process required before a newly added term can be used?
- How are users notified about taxonomy updates?
- Are synonyms handled like preferred terms, or is there a different process for those?

- Do you permit previously assigned terms to be deleted? If so, how do you manage those assets that are now missing a tag?
- Do you permit "root" topics to be assigned? For example, in a taxonomy that includes Animals > Dogs, Cats, Birds, do you permit "Animals" to be assigned as a term?
- Do you permit existing terms to be renamed? If so, do you verify that the renamed terms continue to apply to all assigned assets?
- How do you handle the localization of added or edited terms?

Editing System Configuration

- Who is authorized to make system changes?
- Will you require that system changes be performed on a test system before they are added to the live system?
- How are system changes tested?
- What necessitates a system change?
- When can system changes be made? (Time of day; part of the year, etc.)
- How are system changes communicated to users?
- How can users request system changes?
- Are system changes logged? If so, where, and who can access those logs?
- What is considered acceptable downtime for system changes?
- How is scheduled downtime communicated to users?
- What is the process for handing scheduled downtime that goes significantly past its planned end time?

User Reports and Inquiries

- How can users report problems with the system?
- How can users make suggestions with regard to metadata schema?
- How can users report typos or other metadata errors?
- How can users find help and training?

In reading these ideas, you might be thinking that this all sounds too involved and that it has nothing to do with taxonomy or metadata design, the topic of this book. In fact, taxonomy and metadata are often the only tools users have to comply with policy.

You can see a direct correlation between policy and metadata in examples, such as how you handled a renamed taxonomy term, or how you guide users through the creation of unstructured data. But in a number of other cases, it will be metadata that triggers workflows that deal with many of the back-end policy concerns, such as the archiving of data, or notifications.

Most importantly, though, is that a clearly defined policy helps answer questions about metadata schema when they arise. For example, if policy states that two digital signatures are required before a press release can be made public, your system designers will know that two such fields are required, and they'll know who should have edit access to those fields.

Policy definition takes no time at all when you're *not* thinking it through clearly. And when you *do* think it through clearly, it takes only slightly more time. The entire Additional Policy Considerations section above took me twenty minutes to write. You can likewise quickly come up with a rough table of contents into which you can stuff more details over time.

There's no rule that says your content policy must be complete before your system is launched. But even a basic idea of what your policy will look like will enable you to make a more informed decision about the content management or DAM software you buy, or what's possible with the software you own.

The Value of Synonyms

The nuance of language is what makes it beautiful, interesting, tough to learn, and even tougher to translate–especially for machines. Among the complexities is that we have so many different words that, depending on use or intention, can mean the same things.

You might drive an automobile, a convertible, a hardtop, a coupe, a sedan, a jalopy or even an old clunker. But don't you really just drive a car?

When we're used to a language and its vernacular and idioms, we derive conceptually similar meanings from what can be dramatically different words. For example, if someone says to you, "I drive a convertible," you imagine a car with a removable or collapsible roof. Even though some people refer to a sleeper sofa as a convertible, you gained the "car" context from the use of the word "drive." If that person had said, "I sleep on a convertible," you wouldn't have likely imagined a car, even though a nap in the backseat of a sexy ragtop can be a really nice thing.

Look at that! Turns out you know what a ragtop is too. But your content management system or DAM doesn't–unless you "teach" it to.

Content management systems neither drive nor sleep, so they don't know how to derive those contexts or any others. (Without help from you.) Instead, they accept whatever terms you give them, and they rely on those terms when communicating with users.

This is why careful and strategic use of synonyms is so important.

It's easy for us to become aware of different languages in use around us because, when we hear a language we don't speak, we're aware that something is different. By contrast, when we hear people speaking in languages we understand, we hardly notice them.

We might not expect a Russian native who speaks little or no English to understand what we mean when we say "convertible," but we would expect all fluent English speakers to understand that meaning.

But even within the confines of a single language, there are language barriers. What Americans know as trucks, Brits know as Lorries. And, depending on where you live, what makes those vehicles go is either gas, fuel or petrol.

Even within the same language, same location, and even the same person, there can be differences in terminology. Someone might ask you if there's a chair into which they can sit, and you point them to a stool, couch, sofa, bench or whatever else might be available. Despite having been specifically asked for a *chair*, you infer that the requester's goal is simply to sit.

A content system configured without attention to synonyms might have left the poor person standing forever. A savvy user, though, would have known to try the request again: "Okay, how about a stool or a sofa?"

But this is a game no one likes to play with computers. Synonyms can save your users from this torture, and they'll appreciate it.

And the benefits go deeper too.

Synonyms in Practice

How synonyms are managed depends on the DAM or content management software in use; but support for synonyms should be considered mandatory for any system you consider.

Without synonyms, you'll be forced to add multiple tags to account for all situations. While this is possible, and it is the only option offered by some systems, this isn't ideal because it requires too much work and maintenance.

First off, the tagging user must think of all possible terms that could be applied. Instead of adding the single "car" tag, she would have to think about all those other synonyms users might use when searching for cars. This will most certainly result in metadata inconsistencies because the car images uploaded by Olivia might not get the same tags as the car images uploaded by Hector.

If "car" was the only tag accepted by your system, things would be much more consistent. If Olivia tried to add "automobile," the system would show her the "car" tag instead. She would instantly know that car was the *preferred term* for automobile. Maybe she'd remember that next time, or maybe not. Either way, it wouldn't matter–she'd always be adding the correct tag.

The concept of a preferred term is important when you're looking at a taxonomy organized hierarchically.

Consider the following example:

```
Vehicles
      ↳ Car
      ↳ Aircraft
      ↳ Boat
```

Without synonyms, you'd have (at a minimum):

```
Vehicles
      ↳ Car
      ↳ Automobile
      ↳ Convertible
      ↳ Ragtop
      ↳ Sedan
      ↳ Coupe
```

Worse, you'd have:

```
Vehicles
       ↳ Car
              ↳ Convertibles
              ↳ Ragtops
              ↳ Sedans
              ↳ Coupes
       ↳ Automobile
              ↳ Convertibles
              ↳ Ragtops
              ↳ Sedans
              ↳ Coupes
```

By contrast, if using synonyms, your taxonomy would look like this:

```
Vehicles
       ↳ Car
```

This example shows how the use of synonyms can do a lot of good for the simplification of a taxonomy hierarchy. Does "car" provide the categorization granularity you need? Maybe not–more on that later. But it would certainly make tagging faster and more consistent across users.

Synonyms also offer an important advantage for terms that differ in their singular and plural forms. Goose and geese are completely different search terms, yet a person using one would likely be okay with assets tagged with the other.

Slippery Synonyms

When you start to think in terms of preferred terms and their synonyms, it can become an addictive game: How many synonyms can you come with for each term?

As with the granularity or depth of a taxonomy, you can easily go too deep with synonyms too.

There are two basic branches of "too deep" that apply to synonyms:

- Terms that are homonyms (words that have multiple, completely different meanings) can confuse users
- Terms that only loosely mean the same thing can introduce ambiguity that confuses users

If, while tagging a tree photo, you add the term "bark," what will users think when they're looking for dog photos and they see your tree? We can all imagine the most obvious connection between a dog and a tree (or fire hydrant), but this isn't likely the kind of logic users consider when trying to find photos of Fido.

Likewise if you add "bark" as a synonym to "wood." A user might type "dog bark" into a search field hoping to find images of vocal pooches, but the system displays photos of two-by-fours.

If the system's search behavior default is set to require that all search terms entered be present in the found content, this wouldn't likely be an issue. On the other hand, the system might consider "dog bark" to be the same as "dog wood," which might then return photos of plants too.

The creation of synonyms affects all assets tagged with the preferred term. For this reason, it's important to carefully consider any unintended consequences of synonyms you consider adding.

Synonyms can also introduce ambiguity. Take, for example, "cake." When considering synonyms for this term, you might consider "pie," assuming that baked goods are the goal for any search for "cake." But a pie is no more a cake than a cupcake is a cake. If someone really needed a cake photo, those search results would be annoying.

On the other hand, depending on the expertise and common use cases of your user base, ambiguity might be welcome.

Consider a tomato: It's a fruit, not a vegetable. But does this matter in your system? Perhaps while searching for "red vegetables," it would be okay to show tomato photos because you know that your users are creating brochures, not recipes or culinary lesson plans. (If you fear that someone might put tomatoes into a fruit salad and blame your content system, disregard this advice.)

Ideally, the synonymic relationship between two terms should go both ways. For example, it's safe to assume that all cats are felines, and that all cars are automobiles; but not all boats are ships, and not all trucks are pick-ups. A human male is either a boy or a man; but a male canine is never either.

As a rule, consider whether there might be a hierarchical relationship between any two synonyms you consider. If you find it difficult to make one term subordinate to the other, they're probably good candidates for sibling synonyms.

On the other hand, if a parent/child relationship between the two is clear, you might be introducing problems. For example, all tablets are computers, but not all computers are tablets. This is an example where you might want "Computer" to be a parent term to "Tablet."

As with many topics, the rules for using synonyms in a DAM or content management system can differ from the academic rules that would otherwise apply.

Here are a few considerations to remember when planning your synonyms:

- The goal of a synonym in a content system is to increase the value of search results, not to educate users about language.
- Synonyms should never introduce ambiguity.
- Synonyms that are homonyms should be avoided if their alternate meanings hold some significance to other assets in your system. For example, if your system is about microbiology, chances are, the use of "cell" as a search term won't result in too many jailhouse photos.

Tip: If you like these guidelines, why not make them part of your content policy that governs the creation of synonyms?

When you consider the complexity of dealing with *written* synonyms, imagine how complex things will become when content management interfaces are voice-based.

- flower or flour
- muscle or mussel
- yoke or yolk

Use the nuance of language to your advantage when designing your system. Don't be afraid to break the rules of language when it makes sense to do so.

Your content system isn't about educating users about language; it's about enabling them to find what they need, as conveniently as possible.

Don't forget that machines aren't (currently) too great at deriving context from language. Sentence structure can help engines like Google derive context, but most users don't search in sentences when using a DAM or content management system, which is fine because most such systems don't handle sentences very well.

You'll unlikely account for all adverse situations, which means that you have yet another good reason to make it easy for users to send questions when they arise. If users are ever confused by what they see, they should be letting you know and you should be taking those concerns seriously.

Localization Considerations

When I speak of "localization," I do not mean simple "translation," as in, "What's the Italian word for cupcake?" I refer to taking the *meaning* behind a tag in one language and finding the word in another language that best conveys that meaning to the target user base.

A great example of the problem with (non-localized) literal translation comes from the English term, "mobile phone." When translating this term to German via Google, you get *Mobiltelefon*. But the more common German-language word for mobile phone is *Handy*.

An English speaker might agree that having a cellphone is pretty handy, but if a machine translator was to offer the two terms, chances are the English speaker would assume *Mobiltelefon* was the correct choice.

This matters because *Handy* is the term your German-speaking users are going to use when searching for photos of Androids and iPhones. Upon getting no results, *some* users might think to try *Mobiltelefon,* but using your DAM shouldn't be a game to see who guesses the correct answers; you want to provide the terms users expect.

Then you have your laptop. Google says the French word for this is *portable*, which is sort of easy for an English speaker to imagine–unless, of course you're working on a photograph of someone showing where to place a napkin during dinner. If you're thinking that "lap" would be a safer English tag in this case, Google thinks the French equivalent of "lap" has to do with racing around a track. I guess that makes sense too, but what about the napkin? In fact, I couldn't explain to Google what I meant by "top of the thighs while in a seated position," so I couldn't get the tag I needed.

Asking Google or another translation engine to convert a word or tag from one language into another isn't reliable. If it were, virtually all DAMs would have "Translate Now" buttons in their vocabulary management sections.

The problem is again one of context. Without knowing the context in which a term is used, a machine can easily make bad decisions.

Making matters worse, who will know? If the translation is managed by someone who doesn't speak the target language, bad metadata can be introduced without anyone being the wiser. And, as I've written a million times, bad metadata looks a lot like good metadata, which is why it's so imperative that you not trust automation or any other process that cannot be verified by human experts.

Even if you speak only one language, you've experienced language being used out of correct context. You speak with someone for whom *your* native language is not *his or her* native language, and while you might understand what's being said, you're taken aback at some of the word choices.

I once had a colleague who didn't speak English natively. Understanding his English was no problem–he certainly understood the language well enough to speak it clearly, with competency and authority. But I sometimes found myself temporarily confused in our conversations because of words he used that would momentarily throw me out of the topic.

He told me at the start of dinner one evening that his wife would not be joining us because she was "impaired." This left me wondering exactly what he meant: Did he mean delayed in traffic? Was he opening up to me about some personal problem that prevented her from eating dinner? Was he making an assessment of her mental state?

It turned out, she was sick that day. Is "sick" the same thing as impaired? I guess in some way it is.

Now that my brain knows how to process that word while speaking to him, it no longer throws me. But this is the sort of thing that can make a mess out of a content system's metadata.

The Need for True Multi-language Support

If, at this point, you're thinking that localization is just a matter of adding synonyms in other languages, you're thinking like some software vendors who aim to fool people into thinking their systems properly support multiple languages.

While there are no rules that say synonyms must be in the same language as their preferred terms, relying on synonym support to provide a multi-language content management or DAM experience won't get you far.

User interface language

First off, you have the user interface of the system. If you plan to offer content access to users who don't speak English, an English UI isn't going to be well received. You can add to your English metadata all the Russian synonyms you want, but if Russian users can't use the system, it's not going to do anyone much good.

This isn't to say that you must have UI support for every language you support in metadata. This will depend on your users.

For example, if your users are located in northern Switzerland, chances are the prevailing language is Swiss German. But it's common for Swiss German speakers to also speak French, Italian or English. Because so much of Swiss culture is actually multicultural, "movement" between the various languages is often transparent. It wouldn't be uncommon for northern Swiss users to work in a German-language interface while working with terms in other languages. In fact, if they were required to switch to another UI language each time they wanted to search for a French, Italian or English term, this would be considered an inconvenience.

Unintentional homonyms

Another problem that comes from a system that doesn't offer true multi-language support comes from search mistakes that arise from the same words meaning different things in different languages. We touched upon this before, but the problem is exacerbated when multiple languages are involved.

What do *cane* and *elf* mean?

As an English speaker, the terms might conjure images of things you eat at Christmas and the little characters who deliver them. But to Italian speakers, a *cane* barks, fetches balls and slobbers. Without language context, a content system has no way to interpret the meaning of the search terms provided.

And neither does Google.

The image below shows what happened when I asked the Google Translate service to convert *cane* into German while the "auto detect" option for the input language was selected. I was shown the wrong term because Google didn't know I was "speaking" Italian. After choosing Italian as the input language, I saw the correct result.

Google assumed English was the user's input language (top), so it translated "cane" to "Stock" in German. Once Italian was specified as the user's input language (bottom), the context of "dog" became known and the translation was correct.

If an Italian-speaking user was editing tags in a DAM or content management system and wasn't paying attention, all those dog photos might end up with "Stock" tags assigned.

Also confusing would be when the Italian-speaking user looking for dog photos ended up seeing images of candy canes, walking canes, sugar canes, financial market photos, and shelves of goods in retail stores.

There must be a solid wall of division between the languages supported by your system. Careless use of synonyms can introduce enough confusion within a single language; but synonyms can become a complete mess when multiple languages are concerned.

Ideally, users will be able to choose the user interface language they prefer, and the language(s) that should be considered for the searches they perform.

The value of being able to choose multiple search languages, or being able to tell the system *not* to consider language for a search, comes from terms that should remain the same no matter what the language.

The names of persons, for example, aren't typically localized. So, in some systems, the name might be added to only the primary language of the system. If that means the name was entered in English, and you tell the system you want to search for French terms, you're not likely to find a match.

Some content systems support the concept of a "fallback" language, which means, "if a term hasn't be localized, attempt to find a match on the primary language term." While this can be considered a convenience that saves system managers from having to localize all terms, it can also introduce confusing search results, such as those shown above. Instead of rely on this "lazy person's" feature, it's best to plan a structured localization workflow, as explained next.

Download options

Another popular feature in multi-language content systems is the ability to download a given asset in multiple languages.

In this case, the function is made possible more through an attribute applied to a given version of the content than through any specific metadata value. But a system that does offer this functionality is more likely to truly support multiple languages.

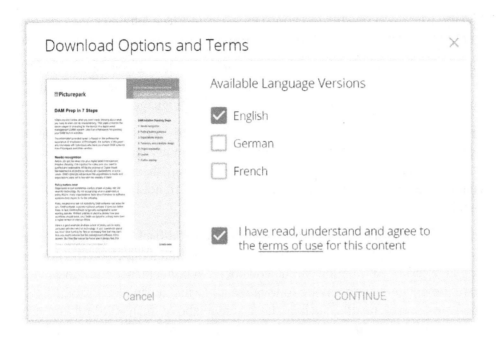

In systems that support multiple language versions, users should be able to choose among the available versions upon download.

Controlling the Localization Workflow

While localizing a single term can present its own challenges, localizing thousands of terms is obviously more complex. Even more a concern is how you'll manage the *ongoing* localization of your DAM or content management system.

Organizations new to content management are often process focused at first, but that enthusiasm wanes after the system has been released. There is always time dedicated to getting the system up and running, but keep it going is virtually never accounted for.

When it comes to managing a multi-language content system, the key is having workflows and policies in place that help you manage the ever-moving target. Otherwise, metadata will become incomplete and user respect for the system will lessen over time.

Chances are you already have at least one business system in place that everyone knows is never up to date. You don't need another.

Also consider localization workflows for regional differences within the same language, such as truck and lorry, as mentioned earlier. In some cases, you should consider same-language "regional localizations" as you would localizations between languages. Though synonyms might be a preferable approach to these situations, you should adopt a localization workflow to make it happen.

Localization policy

Among the questions users might have with regard to localization include:

- Which languages do we support?
- Does all content get localized into all supported languages?
- Do we have to localize all metadata field values?
- How soon after content is added must localization be completed?
- Who is responsible for verifying the integrity of the localized values?

You can use these five items as the basis for developing your localization policy. As you get deeper into the process, you're likely to uncover other questions the policy should address.

Consider the meaning behind each item listed above.

Which languages do we support? This one seems easy, but it's not a decision you can likely make without some input from other areas of the organization.

Among the contributing factors here will be:

- Budget — Do you have the money to do the initial and ongoing localizations?
- Access to resources — Do you have people to do the localizations within budget?
- Time constraints — Can localizations be done in time to ensure relevance? A Twitter feed offers a great example of this concept: By the time you get a tweet about a current event localized into 15 languages, is it still a relevant tweet?
- Need — This decision can be difficult to make. Just because you have an office in Sweden doesn't necessarily mean you need to offer

Swedish as a metadata language in your content system. The majority of employment-age Swedes speak English perfectly well. On the contrary, there are regions of the world in which a single language is pretty much all that anyone speaks. (The United States is a perfect example.) In other places, it would be difficult to choose a single national language based on national boundaries. Consider Switzerland and Canada. And none of this takes into account cultural reasons for choosing a language. If you have an office in France, and you find that your French employees do not enjoy speaking other languages even if they can, you might find that without French metadata, that office will be resist the system.

You'll likely want to discuss language choices with representatives from various departments at your organization. Marketing, Sales and Support are great places to start, especially if your system will be accessible by customers or partners. Find out what languages they speak to the public and ask for opinions about the need for language support in the content system.

Do we have to localize all metadata field values? When creating this policy, you'll be happy to already have a policy that defines the metadata fields in use, because you can simply tack on this requirement to that policy. (Which makes things easier if fields are added later.)

Not all metadata fields need to be *or should be* localized. For example, file names, formats and sizes are what they are. Some of your controlled vocabularies, such as department names, might also be standardized into a single language.

Further, given the complexities of localizing proper nouns or brand names, many organizations leave those alone too. "Disneyland" is pretty much "Disneyland" everywhere. And while there are often localized versions of first names, it's not a standard practice to localize a person's name.

On the other hand, "The New York Public Library" might be unrecognizable as a brand name to users who don't speak English, or those unfamiliar with the region. Further, the terms contained in the name are reasonable search terms on their own, so you might want them localized. Someone who speaks another language who is looking for content about *any* public library in New York, might search using localized versions of "New

York," "public" and "library," without any awareness that the terms form an official brand name.

The examples above offer a good reason why it's helpful to consider localization when developing metadata schemas and vocabularies. If you want to have a policy that says "this field must be localized," you want to make sure that field won't ever contain values that would be difficult to localize.

Unstructured metadata, such as captions, should virtually always be localized. On the other hand, fields you use for internal discussions about content should probably not be included in your localization policy.

Dates also don't need to be localized, unless format is a consideration. For this reason, it's a good idea to use date formats in your DAM that offer no room for ambiguity.

Consider the following:

04-05-2020

Depending on where you are in the world, you'd read that as either April 05 or 04 May. On the other hand, we'd all read this date pretty much the same:

04 May 2020

Granted, in this case, you'd have to consider the localization of the month name. But would likely be handled by your content system as part of user interface language support.

How soon after content is added must localization be completed?
Though none of your content is likely to have the shelf life of a tweet, it's important to have a measurable deadline by which required localizations must be completed. Without such deadlines, you might as well accept that your localizations will never get done because there will always be something more urgent and budget-worthy than metadata localization.

Here are some good reasons for having localization deadlines:

- Automated workflows need specified time frames within which to function. For example, if someone is to be reminded that a localization needs to be done, when would that reminder go out if a date hadn't be specified?

- Users know how long to wait after new content has been added before they should access or share it.
- Deadlines enable you to reign in your localizers so that they know when things are due.

Who is responsible for verifying localized values? There are two things to consider here: Has the localization been performed and is it accurate. In many cases, a single person won't be responsible for both assessments. But your workflows might consider the "is it accurate" to be a sub-task to "is it done." This leaves the ultimate responsibility on the person verifying "is it done" to also make sure it's be done well, or that it's done again.

Localizing newly added content

When adding new content in batches, such as when setting up your system, or after receiving large batches of new content, it's helpful to segment the localization jobs into groups. For example, if your sales materials have priority over archived materials, you'd want to get those done first.

You also want to add flags or other clues to users about which content has been localized and when the rest can be expected. A metadata flag for a localization that's "Pending" enables users to ignore non-localized content in their searches, which might be helpful to them.

Offer a "Localization Expected By" date field to take user experience a step further. This enables users to set reminders for themselves about when important content will be ready for use, and it saves everyone from having to write or answer "when will this be ready?" emails.

"Localization Status" metadata fields make it possible for users to omit from search results any content that has not yet been localized. They also inform users about when localized versions can be expected.

As shown in the image above, you might want to develop notification workflows that alert requesting users or certain user groups when localized content becomes available.

Contrast this to notifications that go out when new content is added: If localized metadata or content isn't usable by a given group, there's no point in notifying them perhaps weeks before they'll be able to make use of the new content.

Managing localization for content newly added to an operational system is actually one of the easier localization considerations. It should be fairly simple to create automated workflows that trigger a new localization process. And with your localization policy in hand, there should be virtually no ambiguity about what needs to be done and by when.

Localization updates

There are situations in which you'll have to reconsider localizations for existing content:

- The metadata has been updated in another language. For example, say that scientists decide that poor Pluto is a planet after all. All those Pluto photo captions will have to be updated again, in all languages.
- Users notice an error with a localized value. (Offer an easy way for them to report such findings.)

New (and admittedly rare) circumstances can affect content in a specific language. The *du-reformen* of the Swedish language in the late 1960s is an example.

- Cultural evolution can result in terms that have fallen out of favor or can even now be considered offensive. Consider Negro > Black > African American, or Eskimo > Native American, or Air Hostess > Stewardess > Flight Attendant.
- Support for a new language has been added to the system.

In all situations, the goal is the same: Launch a re-localization workflow that includes details about what needs to change. Ensure a deadline is given, and that someone verifies the output.

Localization improvements

Given the richness of language, and the fact that localizations are typically done from a single person's perspective, there might be room for improvement.

This isn't to say that certain words are blatantly wrong and should be fixed. But, as you examine the search history for your system, you might find that users are starting to search for terms you (and your localizer) never considered.

The primary difference between this and the "update" workflow suggested above is that, in this case, the catalyst for the update might be simply one person's opinion. A user, for example, might notice a localization that she feels is awkward and can be improved.

There are two nice ways of handling (and even encouraging) this:

- Offer a means for users to offer comments. This has been mentioned several times already, but what's important here is that the context be provided so that the user doesn't have to find a content ID number, then name the metadata field and, finally, explain the situation. That's too much work. Instead, the comment should already identify the asset and field in question.

- Making this even easier for users, your system might support a "suggestion" mode that enables users to edit metadata without making those edits a permanent part of the record. Instead, an admin is notified to consider and approve or reject the suggestions.

Of the two options, the second definitely provides the better user experience. And it will likely result in more suggestions because all you need to say to educate users is, "If you see an error, please click into the field and correct it." The system does the rest. This would be a great addition to your synonyms support too.

Finally, if your localizer isn't a native speaker, considering having a native speaker approve all localizations. This can be done over time so that you don't hold up releases.

Workflow Metadata

When we speak of *workflow*, we refer to a standardized process or a series of steps through which a desired outcome is derived.

As an example, you likely have some routine that starts your day. Shower, brush your teeth, make coffee, etc. This "workflow" might vary some from day to day, but your basic process is one you could explain to or document for another.

You developed the "My Morning Routine" workflow based on experience that taught you which tasks needed to be done in what order to most efficiently achieve the goal of being ready to take on the day. Key motivators contributing to your routine refinement might have been being able to sleep as long as possible, getting into the shower before someone else used up all the hot water, beating traffic, or any other number of things.

At their most basic level, workflows consist of four things:

1. The goal
2. The event
3. The actions
4. Influencing factors

The goal would be what you need to get done. The trigger event is the thing that happens to start the workflow. The action describes the steps you take, and the influencing factors are circumstances that either affect the actions you take or whether you take any actions at all.

Your morning routine can be broken down like this:

- Goal – Get to work on time on weekdays, aware of the day's news, without being hungry or tired

- Event – The alarm clock rings
- Actions – Get up, brush your teeth, etc.
- Influencing factors – Start the process earlier if bad weather might slow your commute; refine actions on weekends when there is no work, etc.

Without even thinking about it, you have built some smart flexibility in this routine. For example, by using the alarm clock as the event, you are able to change the time at which the workflow begins.

Likewise, basing the workflow on actionable, measurable goals enables you to refine the process to account for changing circumstances. Say, for example, that the following day you have a breakfast meeting at a restaurant near your home. You'd considering this when setting the alarm because you might be able to get some extra sleep with a shorter commute and no need to eat beforehand.

We instinctively think about things like goals and motivation when, perhaps subconsciously, designing our personal workflows or routines. But we sometimes have to think about these things more carefully when designing business process workflows that might not yield direct or personal benefits.

You can probably identify a number of workflows you have in your business. Perhaps one workflow is as simple as putting on a headset and clicking a specific button each time the phone rings. In this case, efficiently handling incoming calls would be the goal; the phone ringing would be considered the event; and what you do once the phone starts ringing would be considered action(s). Influencing factors might be if there is someone else to answer the calls; you're on break; the line ringing isn't yours, etc.

The significance of how events and actions relate to metadata will become clear later.

There's nothing magical or terribly interesting about the notion of workflow. A workflow doesn't have to be complex or involve many steps. More complex workflows can often be dissected into smaller workflow building blocks. For example, answering the phone might be considered part of a larger "sales pipeline" business process that includes follow ups, order taking and fulfillment and more.

We make such a big deal about the term "workflow" in content management only because it enables us to describe, build, test and measure *process*, which would otherwise be difficult to manage. If you've read about business process management, then you already have a head start on this topic.

Automated Workflows

When we say *automated workflow*, we refer to a workflow that's carried out by the computer. As with our personal workflows, automated workflows also have goals, events, actions and influencing factors.

Common events in a content system include:

- Content uploaded, downloaded or deleted
- Metadata edited
- Specific metadata field updated to a target value
- Disc space usage increased to or by a given number

The events available to launch workflows will vary between content software. But in virtually all cases, events are based on nothing more than monitoring metadata. (Disc space is more commonly considered "data" than metadata, but if you consider it a descriptor of a storage unit's status, you can see how the term metadata applies.)

Some workflows will be based on time intervals, such as "every 24 hours." And while we might not think of a date-time value as metadata, it's very likely that the workflow itself will edit metadata or at least consider metadata as an influencing factor.

Consider the following examples that could serve as event triggers:

"Assets is ready for archive" — The indication that an asset is ready for archive would most often be a metadata value update made by a user or the system itself.

"Newly added asset needs copyright" — The upload date and current copyright value would be metadata values the system would consider as potential event triggers.

"Asset has been edited" — An asset's modification date is metadata, even though it's not directly edited by users.

One the action side of things are the steps the system should take when the event occurs.

Common actions include:

- Send a notification
- Apply a metadata template
- Archive the content

Just as a ringing phone can prompt you to put on your headset and click a button, newly uploaded content can trigger a content system to apply a metadata template and send a notification.

At the heart of most content management workflows is the monitoring and/or editing of metadata. The connection between workflows and metadata is so important that I would describe their relationship as mutually dependent.

While it's true that some workflows are more about working with content than metadata, any change to content that's not reflected in the content's metadata is a missed opportunity to document the content's history.

If you accept the importance of the connection between workflows and metadata, then it's easy for you to appreciate the value of considering one when designing the other.

Human vs. Machine

It's a desire of many content system designers and users to have the computer do everything, but this isn't practical. Content management software makers tout the value their workflow engines deliver, and integration partners boast about the songs and dances they've gotten systems to do at the flick of a switch. And while some automation is undeniably impressive and valuable, it can become stupid fast.

There comes a point of diminishing return when it comes to developing automation. The problem you face as the person paying to make your system work is that your hired tech crew might be so intoxicated by the notion of experimentation with possibilities that they will accept a challenged based solely on technical theories, rather than considering reality.

Consider the following, increasingly detailed, workflow goals:

- Have the system upload a file on its own.

- Have the system upload a file on its own and tag it based on file type.
- Have the system upload a file on its own and tag it based on file type and uploading user.
- Have the system upload a file on its own, tag it based on file type and uploading user, and notify someone about the new upload.
- Have the system upload a file on its own, tag it based on file type and uploading user, notify someone about the new upload, and enter descriptive tags based on the file's content.
- Have the system upload a file on its own, tag it based on file type and uploading user, notify someone about the new upload, enter descriptive tags based on the file's content, and rate the asset based on presumed popularity that's, in turn, based on the popularity of similar content.

Depending on your perspective as either a content system user or workflow designer, you either read that list as increasingly wonderful functionality, or increasingly absurd user expectations.

Could some software be programmed to do all that? Maybe. The question comes from the value derived versus the effort and expense required to make it happen.

First off, you must consider the trust you place in automation. Some tasks, such as uploading a file, are easy to verify: either the file got uploaded or it didn't. The system does a checksum test to ensure the upload was complete, and you're set.

It's also easy to confirm that tags were added and users notified. If the system is applying the wrong tag for a given file type or uploading user, that's a workflow bug you can likely squash with little effort.

But once you get into asking the system to apply tags that describe content, or rate assets based on some presumed similarity to other assets, things get complicated.

When software compares values, it can make decisions that are basically reliable, assuming the logic in place makes sense. For example, if the uploaded file is of format "TIFF," the system can choose the tag used for TIFF. It can also make presumptions based on its understanding of TIF, such as who should be notified. Likewise, if the name of the uploading user is made available to the system, tagging decisions can be made based on that value.

These are comparison-based decisions, which computers do well. But when you ask a system to make decisions based on the interpretation of content, you're riding the bleeding edge of content management technology.

In general, think in terms of whether an average user could make a given decision with consistent reliability, without training. If the answer is yes, you can probably get the system to do the same. Otherwise, you might be asking for trouble.

Consider this image:

Could your average user tell the following?

- This is a keyboard instrument
- The keyboard casing is made of metal and wood
- The brand of the keyboard is "Moog"

A more trained user might even be able say that this is a Moog Source synthesizer, powered up on program 12 at the time the photo was taken.

The problem is that this isn't a photo at all; it's a 3D render. In other words, there is no keyboard, metal or wood, program 12 or anything else. There is no photographer, no camera model, no shoot date or anything else associated with the photographic capture of a real-world object.

Whoops.

Your automated content management system wouldn't likely have known the difference either. And when it didn't find the embedded (EXIF) metadata it expected from this uploaded "photograph," it would have likely just flagged the content as "missing metadata," and forwarded it to a human for correction. (Photographs taken with modern digital cameras virtually always have embedded EXIF metadata that describes the shoot condition and, by association, identifies the content as a photograph.)

In this case, there was no real error condition. The image recognition technology simply couldn't tell the difference between a photograph and an illustration, so the content system couldn't decide on the correct content class and, by extension, the correct metadata values.

If the inbound metadata included a flag that identified the image as a "3D render," the system could have used that to properly classify it. But this wouldn't be image recognition; this would be good old fashioned value matching, which as we know, computers do well. Further, this would require that inbound content all be properly tagged, which is the very thing fans of image recognition are trying to avoid having to rely on.

You might be thinking, who cares? If the system can tag this as a "keyboard," that's all that matters.

But this isn't good enough for many applications.

Consider the metadata value requirements of different content classes. A "photograph" has a photographer, camera model, shot date, location, etc. A "3D render" has none of those things. Instead, it has an artist (or selection of artists), 3D software name and maybe some other such tags related to a work that is an illustration rather than a photo.

If your downstream workflows rely upon things like photographer name being available for licensing and photo credit purposes, imagine the workflow-stopping confusion when that value wasn't available for this image.

If these considerations were important to you, you'd need verification workflows in place through which the system's content interpretation decisions could be verified. Most likely, these workflows would involve humans who manually check and fix things.

And maybe, at some point, one of those humans asks, "Why don't we just tag these manually? After all, we end up having to fix virtually everything the system does anyway!"

And there you have that point of diminished return. When automated workflows become so complex that you end up assigning human babysitters, you might have over-automated. On the other hand, when automation picks up where human expertise (and availability) ends, you have a nice flow between workflows.

Think 3D vs. photographs is hypothetical science fiction? Ikea catalogs are now made of far more 3D renders than photographs. Read more: http://ikea3d.ContentManagementBook.com

When Ikea catalog designers want to get updated images for next year's catalog, they're not going to want to be delayed because there is no Photographer contact metadata in the content records. This is another reason adaptive metadata schemas are so important: the metadata values available for a given piece of content make sense for that piece of content.

Automated Manual Workflows

Many of the initial workflow goals those new to content management have is the automation of existing manual workflows. Though this doesn't always result in a practical outcome, for reasons mentioned, it is a great way to learn to appreciate the connection between workflow and metadata.

Before attempting to automate any manual workflow, here is the single most important consideration:

Is the manual workflow efficient?

Think back to that example of your morning routine. If you live in a cold climate, one of your morning steps might be, for example, to run downstairs and turn on the heater before you do anything else. This makes sense because it warms up the house so that you're more comfortable performing the other steps of your morning process.

You hate getting out of that warm bed each morning. But you know that if you don't, the house will remain cold, making the rest of your tasks all the more miserable.

You dream of having an automated morning routine management system that can turn the heater on for you. Fortunately, such a system exists; it's called a programmable thermostat. You buy one and promptly set it to turn the heater on at the same time the alarm goes off, so you don't need to run down the frigid stairs.

But even better would be if the computer heated the house *before* you woke up, so you could leave your warm bed without being traumatized. It's a minor detail that makes all the difference, but minor details can sometimes find themselves forgotten when automated tasks are considered.

You'll find that some of your business process workflows involve steps that are no longer valid once content management is in place. So, rather than setting out to automate them, reconsider those manual workflows.

Let's take a look at a common "pre-automation" manual workflow: The Content Request.

A user creating a brochure needs a photograph of the new office building. She calls the company photographer and explains what she needs. The photographer says she can come by to get the photo but she must get permission from the head of facilities before using it.

The designer agrees.

She goes to the photographer's office and gets the photo. She signs a form to indicate she's taking the photo and when she'll return it. As a matter of process, the photographer has already made a backup of the photo, so if the loaned photo is damaged or loss, it won't be gone forever.

The designer places the photo in her layout and then sends a printout of that layout to the head of facilities for approval.

Without getting deeper into this process, let's take a look at the individual steps:

1. Request the photo (designer)
2. Backup the photo (photographer)
3. Pick up the photo and fill out a form (designer)

4. Place the photo and send for approval (designer)

This is a four-step manual workflow that requires only two steps when automated:

1. Download the photo
2. Place the photo and send for approval

Requesting the photo isn't required because it's accessible from within the content system. If the designer has access to the photo via her system permissions, presumably she is authorized to place it in a layout.

A backup of the "loaned" photo isn't required because the original digital file remains in place. So if the designer loses her copy, no harm is done. (A backup of all content in the system is a requirement of system maintenance.)

There is no "loan form" to fill out because the system knows who downloaded the photo, and that one download won't impede others from getting it, if needed. There is no need to return a digital file, so that's not an issue either.

So, before attempting to translate any manual workflow to automation, ask yourself four questions:

1. Is this workflow still needed at all?
2. Are any of the steps of this workflow obsoleted by content management technology?
3. Does the system offer opportunities to do more with this workflow that weren't possible or practicable with manual effort?
4. Will the automation of this workflow deliver clear, sustainable benefits that will justify the cost of automation?

This is an exercise you can do on paper long before you even start working with content software.

That last step is one to consider carefully. For example, if your most aggravating manual workflow involves getting approvals for your annual report, you have to consider the cost vs. benefits of improving that situation. First off, it's something you do once a year. Is it worth improving this rare situation at the possible expense of improving less annoying workflows that happen with more frequency?

Deriving Metadata Requirements

Once you have assessed your manual workflows and decided which are worth automating, you can start to derive metadata requirements from the manual steps each workflow includes. As with the workflow assessment itself, this step doesn't require access to content software of any kind, so you can do it right away.

In most cases, this process is pretty easy and obvious. If you have a workflow that sends an email, for example, you're going to need to know at least one target email address. Or, if a workflow is going to add a copyright notice, you'll need to know what the wording in that copyright notice will be.

Some of the metadata values with which your workflows will interact will be found in your standard metadata schemas. Other values will be supplied by metadata templates, while still others might be calculated or otherwise created on the fly by the workflow.

In some cases, more than one source type might apply. A workflow that takes a date in a metadata field and adds 90 days to that date is one such an example. This could be a workflow that defines "what's new" in your system, with the upload date being the source date and the calculated date defining the expiration of the "new" period.

To determine the metadata values you'll need, you can start by dissecting the plain language you use to define a workflow's goal. There are usually clues in those words.

As a reminder, it's helpful to think in terms of:

- Goal
- Event
- Actions
- Influencing factors

Examples:

Workflow: "Notify sales when new case studies are available"

- Goal: Ensure that sales personnel are aware of new case studies
- Event: Content added
- Actions: Email "Sales" (might be a general email address, or multiple addresses)
- Influencing factors: content type = "case study"

This workflow tells you that you need a metadata content type of "case study" and you need a target email address for your sales team.

Workflow: "Add copyright to newly added material"

- Goal: Ensure copyright notice is available on all content
- Event: Content added
- Actions: Apply metadata template "copyright notice"
- Influencing factors: copyright is empty

Here you can see the need for a copyright metadata field and a metadata template that includes your copyright notice. You might want that template to include a variable for the current year, if that's possible with your system. That way you won't have to update the template each year.

Important note: The logic behind this workflow example is too simple. In practice, finding an empty copyright notice field doesn't mean you can simply claim copyright over the content.

Workflow: "Move old content to archive"

- Goal: Keep "active" part of system free of obsolete content
- Event: Upload date older than x years, or metadata status change to "archive"
- Actions: Remove access permissions for most users; move content to archive storage; update asset reference in content record to point to archive storage
- Influencing factors: Content not marked "Historical Relevance"

You'll already have an upload date, which was provided by the system when the content was added to the system.

You'll need to determine what makes an asset ready for archive. Perhaps that's a value you "hard-wire" into the workflow, such as "180 days" or "5 years," or it could be taken from a metadata field called "Archive By" (date field) or "Archive After X Years" (number).

Using metadata fields gives you some flexibility on a per-asset basis. You might also have a vocabulary-based metadata field called "Status" with which users can force the archive of the content by selecting the "Archive" option.

Optionally, you might have the workflow do nothing if another metadata value indicates that the asset offers some "historical relevance." Maybe this is a checkbox. So long as this value is set, the content will never be archived, no matter how old it gets or what status users select.

Ideally, the content system should disable the "Archive" option in the Status field if this rule is in effect. Alternatively, the workflow should notify the user that the content will not be archived because of the "historical" setting.

Though not related to metadata, niceties like these offer a better user experience and will help avoid support calls by confused users who wonder why the "archive" function isn't working.

Flight Training: Taking the Short Approach   ✕

FLIGHT TRAINING:
TAKING THE
SHORT
APPROACH

Written & Illustrated by David Diamond

ABSTRACT

"Flight Training: Taking the Short Approach" was written as an aviation primer and provides an introduction to the flight training process.

CONTENT STATUS   ☑ Historical Relevance

Status: Current

Archive by: N/A

🖼 Preview   🛒 Add to basket

With "Historical Relevance" checked, this content system shows "N/A" as the archive date, and it disables data entry to the field. This helps users understand why the normal archive option isn't available.

The workflow will also need to know where archive storage is located so that it can move the content there and update the asset record to reflect the new location.

Finally, if you want the workflow to change the asset's permissions so that access is removed for certain users, you'll need to supply those values. How this will be done will depend on your system. For this exercise, though, just note that a permissions change is required.

You'll be able to reconcile your workflow metadata requirements with your standard metadata schema requirements to come up with a complete set of requirements. When a given metadata field is required by a workflow, you might want to indicate that in your metadata schema definition so that others don't question the purpose of the field and inadvertently remove it or change it in some way that breaks workflows that rely upon it.

Common and Useful Workflows

Some workflows are so common that content software provides the functionality outside of the standard workflow engine. This means that you, the user, aren't required to configure anything (much) to gain the functionality.

In some cases, you can build upon one workflow type in order to realize the benefits that a custom scripted workflow would deliver. This can be a big cost savings for you, so take advantage of this wherever possible.

Activating and connecting these flows is metadata. Once you have an idea of what functionality you want the system to deliver, you'll be able to determine the metadata fields you'll need by using a process similar to that described for automating manual workflows.

The most common building block for this concept is the notification workflow.

The notification workflow

In its simplest form, a notification workflow sends an email when some specific thing happens in the system. Example events include content being added, or a specific metadata change, such as a status being set to "Needs Approval."

Some systems can also use the "notification" concept to trigger workflows on remote systems. For example, say a usage restriction notice changes for content that has been placed on a website via integration with a Web content management system. A notification workflow could be used to alert the Web CMS that it should download a "fresh" copy of the content that includes the updated usage restriction in its embedded metadata.

When configuring a notification workflow, the system will want to know what *event* should launch the workflow, what *influencing factors* must be in place for the workflow to run, and what *actions* you want to occur. Despite any fancy user interface the system might provide for making this configuration easy, the fact that you are asked for these three values is your evidence that you are configuring a workflow like any other.

If your goal is something simple, such as notifying your marketing team that new content is available, you'll be able to configure the workflow without adding any custom metadata fields to the system. If you know the team's email address and you know what restrictions you want placed on the workflow, you can set it up in a matter of moments.

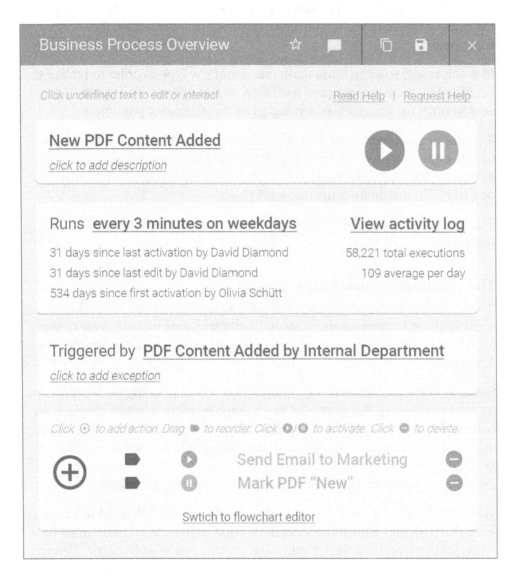

This image shows a means for quickly creating an automated workflow that notifies a marketing team when new PDFs are added to the system.

Though simple by today's automated workflow standards, email notifications can do wonders for an organization's productivity. They become even more powerful when you add custom metadata fields to enable users to proactively interact with the workflows.

The following workflows provide examples of how you can extend the notification workflow to do more.

Review and approval workflows

For some organizations, review cycles require that users comment via overlays that appear on content previews, providing either text notes or simple drawings to communicate with the review coordinator. Some systems provide built-in tools to facilitate this type of review, while some others offer integrations with external tools designed for this purpose.

In some cases, these review and approval tools prove to be more complex than is necessary. First off, they don't work equally well with all content types. For example, you might be able to draw a region over an image and leave a note to "make this lighter." But review options for spreadsheets or audio files are more limited.

Built-in commenting tools become less exciting (and less used) when there are better external proofing tools than those available within the content system. This is the case with Excel, Google Docs, Microsoft Word and PDF, among others.

In the case of Excel, for example, reviewers might need to interact with the spreadsheet in order to ensure it works properly. With Google Doc and Word files, they might prefer the built-in "suggestion" editing options those programs provide. And PDF is known for offering very powerful review options that don't require reviewers to have any special software, beyond the Adobe Reader.

In most cases, a review cycle for these formats (and other non-image formats) involves downloading the asset and opening it in a native application or reader. This, of course, bypasses any review or proofing tools the content system makes available.

Your option as a content system manager is to fight this tide and force users to use the built-in tools, or to enable them to do what works best for them, and just use the content system to provide functionality that is missing from those external workflows.

If you ever make the choice to fight your users, you'd better have a lot of authority and a really, really good reason for doing so. Users always have a way of getting what they want. If they don't, they tend to react by not acting at all.

Users never learn; they only teach: this is one way to look at it.

Fortunately, a combination of the notification workflow and custom metadata can enable you to provide a review workflow that easy for users to understand, and works equally well with all file formats. (Which is to say that, though you might or might not like how it works, it works the same across the board.)

To design this workflow to work for your organization, you need to first decide a few things:

- What are the steps involved with your review and approval workflows? For example, do you have Editorial Review, Managerial Review, In Edit, Ready for Approval? Define those stages.
- Who needs to see your drafts at each step? What you need are email addresses. These can be to individuals or to groups. It's a good idea to use email aliases, even if a notification is to go to only a single person. That way, if that person leaves the company or is otherwise not needed in the reviews, you can adjust that email alias without having to mess with your notification configurations in the content system.
- What constitutes an approval or rejection? For example, do you want to have each reviewer click an Approved or Rejected checkbox? The goal is to make communication easy, so widgets like this can be much more useful than just a Notes field.
- Do you want to enable commenting? In some cases, you might benefit from enabling users to explain their reasons and ideas in a text field. In other cases, you might be looking for a simple yes or no.

What happens next is that you create some custom fields in your system, such as those shown in the table below.

Field Name	Type	Purpose	Restricted to
Review Status	Vocabulary (Pending; Active; Complete)	Enables review initiator to set "In Approval" to launch workflow.	Users authorized to initiate reviews
Editor Approval	Vocabulary (Approved; Rejected)	Enables user defined as "editor" to indicate acceptance	User designated as editor
Manager Approval	Vocabulary (Approved; Rejected)	Enables user defined as "manager" to indicate acceptance	User designated as manager
Editor Notes	Text	Enables user defined as "editor" to provide details	User designated as editor
Manager Notes	Text	Enables user defined as "manager" to provide details	User designated as manager

You can add additional fields for any many other review roles as you need, and you can optionally provide "Notes" fields for each.

If your system supports multiple metadata schemas, this concept becomes much easier. For example, you could define the fields above as being part of a "Press Release Review" content class. When that class was assigned to a given asset, the fields would appear. If the class was not assigned (or was removed after a review was completed), the fields would not be visible.

The added advantage of adaptable metadata schemas is that you can create as many specific review configurations as you need. For example, the review of financial documents, for example, might require a CFO approval that a review of images doesn't require. By creating a "Financial Content Review" content class, all the fields required for that review type would become available.

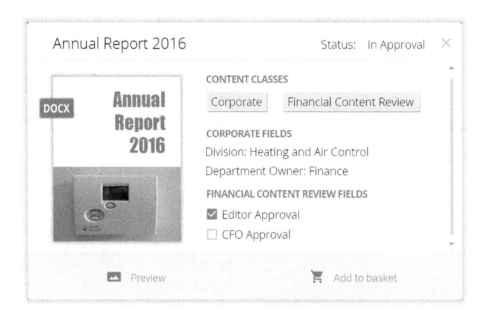

The *Corporate* content class provides fields for division and department owner, while the *Financial Content Review* class provides the fields required by the approval workflow. Once the review is complete, the class (and its fields) can be removed.

Once you have all the custom fields you'll need, you can build your notifications, as shown below. We'll assume that the order of view for this workflow is Editor, Manager and then CFO.

Notification Name	Event (requirements detailed in cells below)	Action
Start Financial Review - Editor	Review Status equals "Active" AND asset class includes "Financial Content"	Notify person designated as editor: "[Document Title] is ready for your approval. Please download, edit with your comments and upload into the system as a new version."
Start Financial Review - Manager	Review Status equals "Active" AND asset class includes "Financial Content" AND "Editor Approval" contains a new value AND new version uploaded	Notify person designated as manager: "[Document Title] is ready for your approval. Please download, edit with your comments and upload into the system as a new version." Notify review initiator: "The Editor Approval from has come in for [Document Title]. The Manager has been notified to start a review."

Start Financial Review - CFO	Review Status equals "Active" AND asset class includes "Financial Content" AND "Manager Approval" contains a new value AND new version uploaded	Notify person designated as CFO: "[Document Title] is ready for your approval. Please download, edit with your comments and upload into the system as a new version." Review initiator: "The Manager Approval from has come in for [Document Title]. The CFO has been notified to start a review."
End Financial Content Review	Review Status equals "Active" AND asset class includes "Financial Content" AND "CFO Approval" contains a new value AND new version uploaded	Notify review initiator: "All reviews are complete for [Document Title]." Update metadata: Review Status set to "Complete"

In summary, by setting the Status field to "In Approval," the review workflow begins:

1. The **editor is notified** to start a review.
2. When the editor uploads a new version of the asset and makes a "yes/no" decision, the **manager is notified** to start a review and the review initiator is provided with a progress update.
3. When the manager uploads a new version of the asset and makes a "yes/no" decision, the **CFO is notified** to start a review and the review initiator is provided with a progress update.

4. When the CFO uploads a new version of the asset and makes a "yes/no" decision, the **review initiator is notified** that all reviews have come in, and the Review Status field is set to "Complete".

If your system doesn't support the updating of metadata from within a notification workflow (which is likely), you could create a normal workflow to update the Review Status field based on all reviews coming in. That, in turn, could notify the review initiator that the review is complete.

The upside of this review cycle is that it's pretty easy to configure and, as mentioned, it works with all file formats.

The downsides, though, are many:

*   There are no reminders to keep the workflow going. So, if the editor forgets to start or complete a review, nothing happens. (A workflow built from the normal workflow editor would, depending on the capabilities of the content system in use, be able to keep track of time and send reminders.)
*   There are no measures in place to account for rerouting. For example, if the system receives a vacation responder or bounce message after sending a "your turn" notification, this should alert the review initiator.

Still, there is a lot of useful functionality delivered here for the cost of a few custom metadata fields.

You can see now why being able to add and remove content classes (groups of metadata fields) would make this process a lot nicer. In the example above, the review initiator could remove the "Financial Content Review" class and all those related metadata fields would be removed, thereby keeping the metadata field view clean.

As an option, you might want to assign field-level permissions to the review fields so that they're visible (and editable) only to the review initiator and the person authored to edit the fields. This would be helpful if you didn't want each reviewer to see the others' comments.

If privacy isn't a concern, you should at least restrict the editability of each review field to the authorized user. This is important because the workflows depend on fields being edited in a certain order. So, for example, you don't want the manager to inadvertently edit the fields reserved for the CFO.

Verifications of taxonomy assignments and metadata changes

Another idea for taking advantage of metadata-based notification workflows is having expert or senior staff verify changes made by less experienced or junior staff.

Most content systems offer only two options when it comes to metadata editing: Either a user has permissions to make changes or not. This was a radically powerful concept when it was first introduced many decades ago in computer file systems, but it doesn't reflect real-world access requirements.

Whether dealing with kids at home or subordinates at work, there is always a concept of "let me check your work" when we're unsure the editor has the information or skill to make a perfect decision. This common sense approach to quality assurance didn't make its way into most content systems, though.

Depending on your system, you might not always be able to easily "roll back" bad metadata edits; but you can at least flag where edits have been made so that a more experienced user can verify the changes made.

This simple workflow example doesn't do anything more than send a notification when certain users make changes. The recipients of those notifications can be then open the edited records and make sure everything looks okay.

Before configuring this workflow, you need to make a few decisions:

- Which users should be "watched"? When these users (or groups) make changes, the workflow will be launched.
- Who should verify the changes made by those users?

If necessary, you can configure multiple iterations of this workflow. For example, you might want one person to check the edits of marketing users, and another person to check the edits of HR users.

Most convenient about this workflow is that you might not need to any custom metadata fields at all. If your system's notification workflows can identify the user who make a change, that's all you need. If not, you might need to add a text metadata field for "Most Recent Editor" and have a workflow add the editing user's name to that metadata field each time the record is saved. You'll then be able to reference that field in your notification workflow.

The logic behind this notification is:

When any record is edited and the editing user is [list of names], send notification to [approver]

This shouldn't take more than a few moments to configure in your system.

If it makes more sense, you can limit the watched metadata fields to only those you feel require verification:

When "Caption" field is edited on any record and the editing user is [list of names], send notification to [approver]

You could optionally modify this by sending a notification when an important field is edited, regardless of the editing user.

Another variation of this workflow is notifying subject matter experts (SMEs) when you need metadata added to or edited on a record verified.

What differs about this variation is that you might want to add "Notify SME" checkbox or other field widget to launch the workflow. When clicked, the workflow launches.

The SME receives an email with a link to the record that needs verification. After confirming the metadata is all okay (or it's editing as needed), the SME can then click another field, perhaps called "SME Verified," that provides a virtual digital signature. Hide this field from anyone who is not the SME, and you have a nice, reliable verification workflow that provides a nice user experience too.

If your system supports multiple metadata schemas, you should be able to assemble the SEM-related fields into their own content class. When that class is added, the fields appear and remain active on the record until the SME has done her job and the fields are no longer needed. If the record is edited again the future, add the class again and the fields reappear.

User-flagged errors, updates or reports

Using a concept similar to the SME review, you can add a checkbox or other field users can click to indicate when they find an error in the content or metadata, or either needs an update.

Again, a system that supports multiple metadata schemas makes this easy because you can group the fields together, so they appear only when an error has been found.

Some metadata fields to consider adding for this are:

- A vocabulary field that enables users to identify the type of report. For example, have they found a metadata error? Does the content need to be updated? Is the content no longer suitable?
- A text field that enables users to explain their findings.
- A vocabulary field that enables the person who will edit the file (the editor) to indicate who he or she is.
- A status field that enables the editor to indicate when a correction can be expected. This is helpful because users can see when to expect an update. If the update is to correct a typo in a sales document, and a marketing person sees that an update is expected by the next day, she might decide to postpone sending campaign that would include the erroneous file.

You might want to limit the visibility of some of the error reporting fields to the reporting user and your editors. (The status and expect-by fields should probably be made visible to all users.)

The logic behind this workflow is simple:

If the "Report" class has been added to the record, notify [some user]

If your system doesn't support adding metadata fields based on classes, you can base the workflow launch event on a value change in one of the two reporting fields.

When the error has been corrected, you can simply remove the "error" class to remove all the related fields, if your system supports multiple metadata schemas. Otherwise, you'd have to manually delete the values in the error fields so that users aren't confused by them.

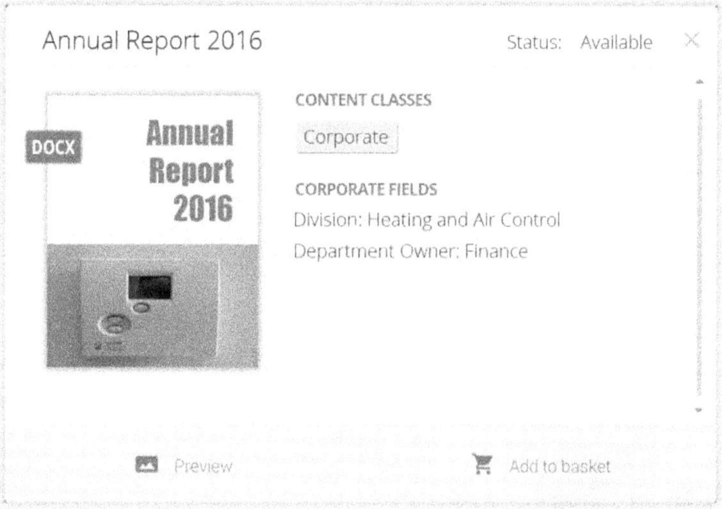

The image on top shows the content record from the perspective of the user who reported the error. Note that only the error reporting fields are editable to this user. Other fields, including those used for the editor's response, are read-only. Below, the Error Report content class has been removed, so the associated fields are also removed. In content systems that don't support adaptable metadata schemas, the only option would be to delete the values in these fields once the error was corrected, leaving the empty fields on the record.

Managing massive tagging projects

Temporary metadata and taxonomy structures can help you manage large tagging projects that might otherwise seem insurmountable. Some of the more common factors that lead to massive tagging projects are:

- Initial migration to content management software — That first move from file server to a content system can be pretty intimidating. Planning the best way to funnel what could be decades' worth of digital content into an organized portal can be tough.
- Seasonal or periodic asset acquisition — For some organizations, there are specific periods of the year during which a mountain of new digital content is created all at once. Seasonal sports organizations, tourism agencies and other such businesses might find themselves inundated with thousands of new digital assets a day, compressed into a short period of time.
- Moving to a new content system — You might think that moving content between systems wouldn't be that difficult. After all, you've already tagged your assets in the older system, so exporting that data shouldn't be that tough. This can be true, assuming you expect no changes in the way you manage all that metadata. But in many cases, the reason organizations move to newer content management systems is to take advantage of new functionality. This results in a migration that is part metadata-move and part metadata-make.

There's no getting around the fact that projects like these can take considerable time; but some organizations find they spent more time wondering how to get started than they did executing a good process.

Auto-tagging

Here are a few (unofficial) classifications of metadata auto-tagging, in order of increasing sophistication and decreasing reliability:

- Extraction
- Deduction
- Guessing

Extraction refers to a content system's ability to "look" inside an inbound file for embedded metadata values, and pull those values into the system. These values are stored right inside the file itself, so anywhere the file goes, so goes the embedded metadata.

The metadata found inside a file depends on a number of factors that are unfortunately not predictable. Of those factors, most relevant is file format. Only certain file formats support the embedding of metadata, and virtually all of those files are image or audio formats.

There are embeddable metadata standards, such as EXIF and IPTC Core, for which standardized metadata field schemas are published, but there is no guarantee that all metadata values defined in the standards will be embedded into the files you bring into your system. In fact, you can be virtually assured that at least some or most values will be missing.

What this means is that, though you most certainly want to take advantage of metadata extraction where you can, you cannot assume it will be enough to properly and completely tag inbound content.

Also included with standard metadata extraction is the ability to pull in metadata that's not file-format dependent, such as file name, size, format, modification date, etc.

The next level in auto-tagging sophistication would be to have the content system make some decisions about tags based on extracted metadata. This is a fairly simple rules-based approach to auto-tagging.

Here are some examples:

- If the file format is JPEG or TIFF, and the file name contains "cup," add tag "Tableware"
- If the file format is PPT or PPTX, add tag "Presentation"
- If Copyright does not include {our company name}, add tag "Licensed"

A rules-based approach like this can help provide a number of useful metadata values. But you can probably imagine there could be some reliability issues. The first bullet point above, for example, would be problematic if your system was used to manage, in addition to photos of coffee cups, photos from the World Cup.

The most sophisticated auto-tagging falls into the "guessing" class. Here, we speak of a computer's ability to recognize faces, dogs, famous landmarks and other such shapes for which it can associate a tag.

We've seen some impressive examples of this technology, but it's not yet perfect. In some cases, for example, the computer can tell there's a dog in a photo, but it doesn't know the dog's name, and it can't tell the difference between two dogs that look similar, a male versus a female or, in some cases, live versus stuffed.

And then there's the consideration of vocabularies versus image recognition algorithms. If your business is veterinary science, the "dog" tag offers limited value. You likely have a vocabulary that contains scores of breed-specific tags that are important to what you do. Unless you could "teach" the technology to provide the differentiation that's important to your work, you might find the auto-tagging option to be little more than interesting.

Rest assured, we can expect auto-tagging technologies to become increasingly useful, but for now, be careful. Bad metadata looks a lot like good metadata, so you want to make sure you don't introduce both into your system. (More on this later.)

Adding human resources

With the romance of auto-tagging magic in your rearview mirror, your next idea might be to hire additional resources to help get you over the hump of a big project.

While this might be a costly option, it can be the best option. But the best way to go about it might not be apparent. First off, let's look at some *disadvantages* to letting larger projects drag on:

- The fuller value of the content system as an archive is delayed until the project is complete. This can result in a reputation with users of the resource being of limited value, even long after this is no longer the case.
- When a one-time project takes too long, it can become entangled in maintenance projects, such as annual metadata reviews. The result can be mass confusion about what's new and what needs to be updated.

- Despite your best documentation efforts, the people in charge of your large tagging projects will always know best what's going on. If one (or all) of those people leave, you're going to lose valuable time.
- Content systems that take a very long time to get launched are more likely to never get launched because enthusiasm and budgets can wane.

There are other considerations too, but these examples are easy to appreciate and easy to explain to those who might be holding the keys to your budget for additional staffing.

Typically, when an organization considers temporary help, they think in terms of interns or other lower-wage workers whom they can fit into budget scraps they find lying around. Though I'm not going to tell you this is a *bad* idea, I am going to tell you it's an *incomplete* idea.

Depending on the complexities of your content collections and the search terms users are expected to use to find that content, untrained workers might not be able to tag things correctly.

Consider the following photo:

What tags would you expect from an untrained intern? Probably most would come up with the following:

- Post Office
- Cafe
- Parking
- Sign

Some might additionally suggest:

- Daytime
- Sky
- Trees

Not coincidentally, these would also be the tags you might expect a computer to be able to generate on its own.

But what about less obvious or literal attributes of this photo?

- Small town
- Hand-painted
- Bolted
- Wooden

You might not expect your intern to think of these tags, but they could be useful in search. You might also want to know what kind of trees those are in the background. (I wanted to show off and mention the kind, but I have no idea.)

Taking less obvious attributes further, this sign is from a parking lot in a small Northern California town called Cromberg. The location might be of no consequence to your needs for the photo, but if it were, you'd need an intern who knew.

Now, multiply the needs for that photo by the million or so assets you might have to tag, and you can see how "cheap" labor alone is not going to get you where you want to be.

Subject matter experts (SMEs) can get us "the last mile" with regard to tagging authority and completeness; but, as you can imagine, they're not cheap and they're not plentiful.

Fortunately, there is a way you can use junior labor alongside experienced labor to get you where you need to be.

Tagging in concentric circles

The first part of this book included examples that suggested a child could differentiate between photos of obviously different objects. That same concept is a secret weapon you can use in your larger tagging projects.

Tagging can be done in cycles, with the first cycle offering the most general (and obvious) tags, and subsequent cycles being used to add increasingly finer details. Though it might seem disadvantageous to consider each asset more than once, there are significant benefits to this approach:

- Less skilled (and more affordable) workers can do the "broad strokes" tagging.
- More skilled workers can focus on details, without having to add all the obvious tags, which is a better use of their time.
- More than one subject matter expert can be employed and called as needed, which enables you to take advantage of detailed expertise more efficiently. (And having the basic tags done, it's easier to assign content to the correct SME.)
- An incomplete content system can be launched sooner because there are at least some metadata values in place with which users can find the content.

A few variations on the notification workflow already discussed is all you need to make the "concentric tagging" workflow work. First off, you'll need to add some custom metadata fields to help your team manage the process. The following table outlines some suggestions.

Field Name	Type	Purpose	Restricted to
Tagging Stage	Vocabulary (Pending; Level 1; Level 2; Complete and Verified)	Enables users to see the current status so they'll know what to expect. It also serves as a bookmark for what needs to be done.	Users authorized to manage tagging
Level 1 Tagger	Vocabulary (Names of Level 1 taggers—your junior workers)	Enables tagging managers to assign and review taggers	Tagging managers
Level 2 Tagger	Vocabulary (Names of Level 2 taggers—your subject matter experts)	Enables tagging managers to assign and review taggers	Tagging managers
Level 1 Notes	Text	Enables user defined as "Level 1 Tagger" to communicate to tagging manager	User designated as "Level 1 Tagger"
Level 2 Notes	Text	Enables user defined as "Level 2 Tagger" to communicate to tagging manager	User designated as "Level 2 Tagger"

Level 1 Status	Vocabulary (Pending; In Progress; On Hold; Complete)	Enables user defined as "Level 1 Tagger" to keep track of her progress on each asset	Tagging manager and Level 2 tagger (in case Level 1 tagger leaves a note important for the Level 2 tagger to see)
Level 2 Status	Vocabulary (Pending; In Progress; On Hold; Complete)	Enables user defined as "Level 2 Tagger" to keep track of her progress on each asset	Tagging manager

Collectively, these fields provide some useful information and interaction capabilities:

- All users see the general tagging status of all content, which enables them to "trust" the content to lesser or greater degrees.
- Tagging managers additionally see the "level" specifics for the content, which enables them to monitor progress, visually verify the work for each tagger, and better estimate completion dates.
- Taggers can see what they need to do, and keep track of status of the content they're working on. If, for example, they need help with some piece of content, then can set it to "On Hold" until they get the information they need. That way, they can move on to other content without having to maintain an external list of which content is incomplete.
- The various "Notes" fields enable taggers to communicate with managers.

Tagging workflows can be managed by metadata fields that help users track and see the status of each round within the workflow. In this image, Level 1 tagging is complete; Level 2 tagging is underway. Once tagging is complete, the *Tagging Workflow* class and its associated fields are removed.

With these fields in place, you have the mechanisms you need to build a few useful workflows, and you can make some decisions with regard to system policy.

- Should content be released after Level 1 tagging is complete? If so, you can build a workflow to update the permissions on content for which that stage is complete.
- When taggers are assigned, email notifications can be sent.
- Level 2 taggers can be assigned via "bulk editing" that's based on searches that find like content. For example, "find all airplane content" and then assign them to your aviation subject matter expert.
- Saved searches can be configured to enable taggers to always see what needs to be done.
- Saved searches can be configured to enable tagging managers to see what's been done recently.
- Level 2 taggers can be notified when Level 1 tagging is complete.
- Tagging managers can be notified when Level 2 tagging is complete, so they (or others) can verify that all tagging is complete.
- Users can be notified when tagging is complete for content that interests them.

You'll likely be able to imagine other workflows that could be enabled by these metadata building blocks.

If your system supports adaptive metadata schemas, this is an obvious use for that technology. If this isn't an option, make sure you can at least adjust permissions so that general users don't see the workflow fields they shouldn't see. If that isn't an option, you'll want to reconsider taking an approach like this because it's too likely that casual users will inadvertently edit one of the workflow fields, which will result in confusion.

A variation on this set up would be to *not* assign Level 1 taggers specifically, but permit a team to perform this function and then select their own name from the "Level 1 Tagger" menu as a means for taking responsibility for the record. (Perhaps you offer some incentive for tagging, so that a group of users proactively looks for content that needs Level 1 tagging.)

Launch plan for an incomplete system

If you wait to launch your content system until it's done, you will never launch. The very nature of content management is that it's always a work in progress. Even if you don't plan to be adding new content regularly, you might discover new ways to manage the content you have.

What's more, because content management is a considerable expense, it's a good idea politically to show value for that investment as soon as you can. We've all seen corporate projects that dragged on for so long that they were long forgotten before they ever saw the light of day.

This happens with content management initiative planning too.

So it's a good idea to plan to launch an incomplete system. The trick is to handle the lead up to the launch, the launch itself, and subsequent updates efficiently and effectively.

Knowing you won't launch a complete system, think about how you can make an incomplete system usable. For example, when building a house, there are many things that can be left unfinished while still making the house habitable. You don't need exterior paint or landscaping before you move in, but you do need floors and a roof.

You can apply similar concepts to the construction of your content system and the addition of your content. Always think "users first" when deciding how to prioritize and manage things.

With regard to the system itself, here are some things you might be able to delay, if necessary:

- Custom, purpose-specific user interfaces (such as mobile access portals) might not be needed until you have more content in place.
- Content processing (conversion) configurations that aren't needed at first.
- Workflows that run only periodically, such as quarterly or annually.
- Workflows that perform functions that are more convenient than necessary.
- Integrations into other business systems.

You'll have to speak to your system configurers to determine what time savings there might be by delaying these or other aspects of the system. In some cases, the savings might be minimal. In other cases, delaying one aspect of the system might be a bad idea due to interdependencies with other parts of the system.

You absolutely do not want to postpone any functionality that will affect metadata quality or usability. For example, if your metadata schema designs require workflows to validate user input, or calculate values based on user input, those workflows should be in place at launch or else you risk having bad or incomplete metadata that's not part of a managed update.

You also don't want to compromise on user experience. Many users new to content management will approach your new system with the same enthusiasm they have for dental checkups. Give them any reason to not come back and they'll take it. This means that interface functionality should be in place and working, online help should be available, and policy should be clear and well communicated.

There is no doubt that you'll come up with ideas for improvements after launch, once you see how users respond to the system. But this isn't justification for releasing something that's half-baked and barely usable.

With regard to the prioritization of adding your content to the system, I've seen three areas of focus work pretty well:

- By content type
- By year
- By department

The primary advantage to each of these is that they are easy for users to understand. For example, "all sales materials will be in the system by the end of March."

Adding content by year is most valuable for systems that will serve as historical archives. For some organizations, it makes the most sense to start with the current year and work backward; others prefer to start at the beginning and work forward. In either case, the benefit is that users will know what they can expect to find and what's coming next.

Adding content by department means you consider all the content that Marketing uses, that used by Sales, that for Legal and so on.

This option offers an additional important advantage: user training. Once you add all the content for Legal, you can then schedule training for the users in that department. Because they will all likely have a similar use case for the system, you can tailor your training to speak to them using language and examples that are clear to them.

Department-based deployment is especially important when you need to train users worldwide, because "speaking their language" could become a literal benefit.

In each of these cases, an incomplete system can still offers users a complete benefit.

There are no specific metadata requirements to partial deployment by content type, date or department, because the content you haven't added isn't there to be noted as "to do."

If you will be providing different taxonomies for each department, for example, you'll of course want to make sure those are in place before they're needed. You'll also need to update at least a few of your controlled vocabularies to account for the content that's coming next.

You can read more about deployment ideas and recommendations in DAM Survival Guide. Though the book speaks specifically about digital asset management systems, the concepts are applicable across other content management systems too. (As mentioned, they're rapidly becoming the same thing.)

Metadata and Taxonomy Reviews

By conducting periodic metadata and taxonomy reviews, you'll be able to:

- Study users' reactions to what's in place now to see what's missing or misunderstood.
- Realign your metadata schemas with evolving policy or administrative needs at your organization.
- Compare user search histories with existing metadata to see whether people are searching for the terms you expected.

Depending on the size of your organization, you might want to assemble a metadata review panel to assist in the process. Having someone on hand who represents each stakeholder group can be helpful, both practically and politically.

If you do plan to have a panel, consider assembling it before your system launches. This provides you with a few benefits:

- You won't be accused of playing favorites with your panel member selections. If you wait until after the system is in use, people might think you asked those who were already fans of the system. After all, would you really want to ask someone who always complained?
- You can use your panel members as evangelists for the system. They can promote it to their respective constituents, which might increase adoption.
- You can schedule your reviews months in advance, which means your team is more likely to actually conduct the reviews.

For a new system, you might want to schedule metadata reviews for 6 months, 1 year and 2 years after launch. Your 6-month review should be focused on user input about what fields people think are missing or misconfigured, and what they don't understand about the metadata schema.

As mentioned, it's always a good idea to have an easy means for permitting users to make suggestions or ask questions. Your team can consider this initial input at the 6-month review, and plan any changes you deem fit.

After the system has been in use for a year, you'll have more search data that you can compare to available metadata values. You'll also likely have more content in the system. At this review, you'll be targeting your vocabularies, with specific attention paid to your synonyms.

For the record, the search data we speak of here has nothing to do with the Web browser histories of your users. Your system should be tracking the terms people search for and, subsequently, the content they access. User account data might or might not be associated with the search history—this will be system dependent.

The idea is to see if you find gross mismatches between search terms and resulting user actions. Common areas where you might find disconnects include:

- Spelling mistakes or variations — If you find repeated examples of people searching for *chanukkah* and *xmas*, and your system uses the tags Hanukkah and Christmas, consider adding as synonyms the terms people are using.
- Terms not considered in metadata — When you see the search history, you might recognize terms you forgot to add as primary metadata tags or synonyms.
- Terms with no associated assets — In some cases, you might see reasonable search queries and realize you have no suitable content or, for whatever reason, the content you do have isn't being found. This can suggest metadata input mistakes. In either case, you can decide what to do. Maybe you need to license some new material or have an in-house person create the missing content.
- Terms that find assets but result in no record views or downloads — If a given search term finds assets in your system but you see in the

activity logs that most users end up searching again right afterward, the problem might be false positive matches. In other words, the system is finding the wrong content, as far as users are concerned. Some "fingerprints" that suggest this is happening are searches that result in no record views or downloads, and repeated searching in a short period of time. (Exactly what happens when you can't find something using Google — you try alternate terms without clicking any links.)

The 1-year period is also a great time to survey your user base to see what they think in general. Shorter surveys are usually more likely to get completed, so you might want to limit what you ask to a few simple questions:

- In general, how useful do you find the system?
- How often do you find what you need?
- Do you have ideas for the system that you'd like to share?

The first two questions could be handled with a 1 - 5 rating system. The last question is your clue as to which users should be on your radar. Those who want to share ideas should be contacted. Their ideas might be good and you might even turn these users into evangelists for the system.

Try to avoid questions you don't need to ask, such as "How often do you connect to the system?" or "How many pieces of content do you download content from the system each month?" Your system statistics should be able to show you this, and users won't reliably remember these values anyway.

The action items from your 1-year review are likely to be much more involved than those from the 6-month review, so plan accordingly.

Consider your 2-year review more of an assessment of the burgeoning maturity of the system. By this time, you should have a good handle on what users are searching for and what the system is delivering to them. Your metadata schemas should be relatively stable and your users should be pretty well trained.

Depending on the shape of things at the two-year point, you can decide when your review panel should meet next.

In the meantime, conduct your own periodic spot-check reviews of what's been recently added or edited. If you see a consistent error, consider why.

Don't get too far behind on user input. Keep users informed about what you're doing, when you're doing it and why it's being done.

Future Metadata

Much of this book and other discussions about metadata are about ways to maintain metadata integrity. And while there's no question that the integrity of metadata is important, the industry is trending in a direction away from absolute fact, toward opinion and assumption.

One needn't look any further than Wikipedia to see where this trend originated. Inherent in the Wikipedia content model is a flaw that makes it too easy for incorrect data to find a permanent home alongside correct data. The problem lies in *sources* or, in the case of Wikipedia, a lack of reputable sources.

Wikipedia topic editors provide the information (they think) they know and, in many cases, they refer to other Internet articles as proof of the claims they make. External articles, of course, prove nothing other than what's claimed in the Wikipedia article has been claimed elsewhere. But this isn't proof and it certainly isn't the fact checking we learned to expect from the publishers of reputable printed encyclopedias.

Still, this "fuzzy" approach to documenting the world's knowledge works in many cases. For topics that are widely studied and understood, errors are usually found, and claims can be challenged. One can assume that from these challenges comes a more accurate "truth."

Take the Christian bible, for example. This is a book known by billions of people over the ages. It's studied, localized into different languages, and taken to be "the word" by many. Even with all this scrutiny, though, there are "believers" who argue the meaning behind passages within the book. But thanks to globally accepted knowledge on the subject, publishers are able to print editions that are considered to be basically accurate.

Unless, of course, you don't believe that any of what's said in the book is anything more than total fiction.

The fact is, none of us today were around in the days the book describes. We have no firsthand accounts of any of it. We don't even have great-grandparents who can attest to it. Some have "faith" that the book tells of accounts that actually happened; others laugh at the stories within; others make public policy based on it; and still others war over it.

Now imagine what happens when, in a few decades, people look back at what we're today turning into our societal sources of fact and ask, Says who? Will blog posts become the "historical" references future articles cite?

For topics that are not widely understood or known, misinformation can make its way into the public consciousness even faster. In fairness, you'll see "[citation needed]" alongside statements in Wikipedia for which no concrete evidence has been provided, but this doesn't solve the problem. People still take information they find in Wikipedia and speak about it, or publish it elsewhere as fact. The "[citation needed]" disclaimer seems to be all but invisible when people want answers.

"It must be true, I saw it on Facebook like a bazillion times."

Before long, thanks to article after article, the propagated misinformation is what you find when you search Google, and the process of rewriting history is complete. Few people think to question what Google Search shows them.

I've written more on this topic. (Search "What Happens When Google Says No - DAM Survival Guide") If you think such a thing can't happen, you'll want to read that article.

Asking Experts

Perhaps in response to our daily inundation of what we know to be falsities or partial truths, we have increasingly turned to subject matter experts (SMEs) for clarification. We see SMEs on news programs, lecturing at universities, consulting at organizations and, as suggested earlier in this book, editing metadata.

It's great to have someone who can bring to light the facts. But have you ever found yourself listening to an SME and either had a feeling he was wrong or, worse, *knew* he was wrong?

There is no "Subject Matter Expert" school or standardization. Like "Consultant," holders of the title "expert" vary wildly in the value they deliver. You might encounter SMEs you find to be worthless, and you might find people who don't even consider themselves SMEs to possess a wealth of knowledge about a given subject.

Even after you've found an SME you trust, there comes into a play another consideration: opinion vs. fact. The very purpose of an SME is to fill in the blanks where facts aren't apparent or complete. This means, by design, that opinions enter the fray.

In some cases, the SME will willingly speak almost entirely in opinions (as I do in this book); in other cases, an interviewer will solicit opinions from a reluctant subject. Typically following an SME who says, "I wouldn't want to speculate," an interviewer follows up with, "Yes, but certainly your experience must leave you with *some* ideas."

The SME's ideas are presented; viewers take them away as fact; headlines quote them; and you have what is, at best, factually soft news.

But "basically true" and "seems like it is true" is what we're used to now. In many cases, an SME's ideas are far more entertaining than the truth, assuming the truth ever presents itself. And SME ideas and opinions are always more interesting than having nothing to report. So we have learned to accept that our news sources often have no factual sources of their own for the "news" they report.

Fuzzy Logic means Fuzzy Metadata

"It seems to me" and "I think" are phrases we use to soften the value of our opinions on topics. We even have the word *circa*, which conveniently enables us to approximate dates. So, it's not like we've been slaves to fact forever. But we're taking this "softness" further now and, in most cases, we're no longer qualifying any lack of certainty.

Ask someone if she believes everything she hears on CNN or the BBC and she'll likely say no. Then ask her if she has ever re-shared anything on Facebook that she hadn't first verified to be true.

In many cases, "I like what's being said here" is the only determination we use for what we "like" and re-publish across our social channels. In many cases, people don't even read the article behind the link, so long as they find the headline agreeable. (Even more likely if we know and respect the original publisher–it's that SME thing again.)

If you're curious about what news sounds like when it's not rife with speculation, ideas and opinions, consider this:

"Earlier today, a Malaysia Airlines Boeing 777 departed from Kuala Lumpur International Airport. The flight, call sign MH370, was scheduled to land in Beijing Capital International Airport. The airplane never arrived. Search crews continue to look for clues as to the aircraft's whereabouts; but, at this time, no cause for the disappearance is known."

There you have it: the breaking story, as reported using just the facts. Not much value to a 24-hour news cycle. So, within no time of the initial reports, we saw flight paths, cockpit photos of pilots with women guests, speculation of terrorist affiliation, theories about why transponders would be deactivated, and a mountain of other information that, to this day, has yet to prove relevant.

I mention these things because a fuzzy approach to accuracy is where metadata is headed too.

Euphoric enthusiasm for imperfect auto-tagging technologies, combined with the seemingly insurmountable task and expense of properly tagging massive collections, has left people wondering just how bad it would really be if the metadata wasn't perfect.

Given the time savings, couldn't we live with a few errors? For some (many) organizations, the answer is yes.

Google Photos introduced an auto-tagging technology that was far from perfect, but it was so impressive that we collectively bowed to it and salivated with anticipation for the next version, which we expected would be absolutely perfect.

But even in its imperfect 1.0 state, it saved people time. I know virtually no one who manually tags personal photos now. Are the tags as precise as they would be if tagged manually? No. But the photos are tagged, which is something that might not have happened had it been up to the individuals.

In addition, as time goes by, a new generation of customer becomes the company's focus. And much like "grownups" today don't much care about the quality differences between typewriter ribbon brands, this new generation of Google customer looks at the tone of Old School, fact-based news as bland.

Where we were once uninformed, looking to be educated; now, we're bored, looking to be entertained.

Personally, being used to what good content management technologies can offer, I actually see Google's early offering as little more than entertaining. When I search for "dog" in my Google Photos collection, it amazes me that it finds photos with dogs, even if one of those dogs is actually a stuffed toy.

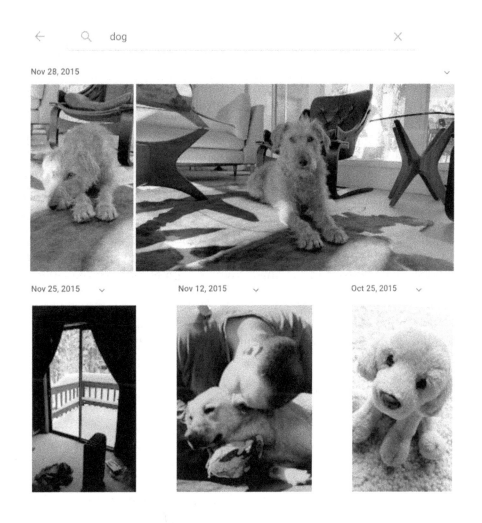

Google Photos finds real dogs, stuffed dogs and a snow-covered balcony upon which no dog can be seen.

Granted, the "dog" results also include a photo of snow on a balcony, upon which there is no dog. (Though, the stuffed dog was actually *behind* the camera in the balcony photo, so maybe Google Photos is more magical than I think.)

But when I search for "car," the results are confusing. At the top of the results are photos of me at the top of a ski mountain. I can't be certain, but I'm virtually certain I took the gondola up the mountain that day and left my car in the lot. The mountain is in Truckee, California, though. So perhaps there was some association between Truckee, trucks and cars? (I see those same ski photos when I search for "food." Yes, there is a restaurant at the top of the mountain and, yes, we are what we eat. But really? Food?)

Further down the search results, I do see some car photos, but not all of them. Google tends to favor photos of my Audi over those of my Chrysler—a preference I find difficult to argue.

But mixed within the results are photos of my friend, Tony, swimming across Donner Lake while training for a marathon. I was spotting him in a kayak. Perhaps Google mistook his wetsuit for rubber and assumed he was a swimming tire?

Look, I don't mean to badger Google or any other company working on advancing technologies—I applaud them for moving things forward. But they are introducing a "new normal" for us, with regard to how we see and appreciate data.

There was a time when we would have just said the search results are wrong, and left it at that. Now, we ignore what's wrong and beam with excitement over what it got right.

"Look! It found my dog photos!"

Now type in your dog's name and search again.

Before moving on, let's review some of what's been discussed in this section:

- When misinformation is propagated enough, people accept it as fact. Wikipedia and Google Search have shown us this.
- When auto-tagging technologies are used, a certain error rate can be expected—no one disputes this, even the creators of the technology.

- When people are enamored with a new technology, they tend to forgive it more than will people years into the future. Dropped calls on early cellphones were an exciting reminder that we were wireless. Today, they're grounds for switching carriers and venting hysterically on Twitter.

Given these considerations, are you really willing to introduce metadata into your content system that isn't 100% perfect?

Probably you are; it seems most organizations are. So, at this point, I'll stop fighting the trend, and discuss it from the perspective of one who champions the idea.

Because, believe it or not, I do.

Making Metadata Intriguing

What benefit could there possibly be from metadata that's less factual?

First off, *relevance*.

This isn't to say that facts aren't important–I'm still a believer in the truth. But much of the value derived from metadata doesn't always have to be about facts; it can be about opinions, stories and other "unprovable" anecdotes.

Say, for example, you have digital copies of works by Picasso, Da Vinci, Monet and Van Gogh in your museum's collection. You're about to launch a new Web-based exhibit that will feature these digital works.

The metadata records for each would likely contain a title, year, period, the artist's name–you know, the basic *facts* you would find on an information card at a physical exhibit. You would certainly want this information to be accurate, but would this information be the reason people would stop by to see the exhibit?

Now, imagine someone has the idea to add to that metadata. "Let's get the opinions from famous people who were inspired by these artists," she suggests.

Imagine the response to an ad that reads:

"Find out why Madonna hates Picasso, and how Queen Elizabeth thinks Leonardo da Vinci missed his true calling."

All of a sudden, you have metadata that is not based in fact, but provides great relevance. What's more, it's unique metadata that wasn't available before, and that will become a permanent part of the history of each work.

In other words, you are no longer just *presenting* history, you are *creating* history.

(For the record, I have no idea what Madonna or Queen Elizabeth think of Picasso, da Vinci or anything else. Please do not commit this to your brain and one day say at a cocktail party, "You know, I read somewhere that Madonna hates Picasso." If I read this one day on Facebook, I'm going to be pissed!)

We are becoming a society increasingly driven by interest in personal experience. Reality TV and Facebook prove to us that a story doesn't need to be universally epic for us to pay attention. I think we could agree there are today millions more people interested in what Adele thinks of anything than there are people interested in the date something was painted.

We shouldn't discard the tide of public interest when considering what's relevant metadata wise. Let future curators of your collection accept or disregard what they will; in the meantime, you have an audience to consider, and that audience is currently all about entertainment.

Multiple Metadata Profiles

Another advantage of where we're headed is that we're going to see many different metadata profiles for any given piece of content.

For example, Switzerland's Matterhorn would be a very different metadata discussion, depending on your perspective. Are you selling expeditions or are you a geographer? Maybe you maintain a website of the world's most popular ski resorts and all you care about are ski lift hours of operation, and nearby hotels.

Depending on our perspectives, there is information we want to know and information that offers us no value. But it's all metadata.

The concept of different content systems having different metadata schemas isn't new—in fact, virtually all DAM and content management system installations have different metadata schemas.

But there are two situations that are, in fact, fairly new:

- Multiple metadata schemas across departments
- Multiple metadata schemas for "linked" digital assets

In the first case, we speak of the same content being represented by multiple metadata schemas within the same organization. For example, a photo of your office building has different value to those in Marketing than it does to those in Facilities.

Marketing might use the photo in brochures and advertising. Among the metadata values they'd like know are:

- Image size
- Color space
- Campaign use history
- Photo credit
- Shot conditions (was it a nice sunny day?)

One could look at these fields and derive that those in Marketing have some interest in the actual content. After all, they will be placing it in layouts and publishing it, so they need to know things like how big it is or who needs to be credited for its use.

On the other hand, the folks in Facilities are thinking more about:

- Location
- Square footage
- Building manager
- Exterior paint color code

It's fair to say that these folks are more interested in the subject of each photo than they are the file itself.

Same photos; different perspectives.

Content systems that support adaptive metadata schemas make managing multiple metadata schemas like this possible, if not easy. Each schema layer can be thought of from the perspective of the state of the content, different stakeholders' perspectives and needs, and more.

Systems that support only a single metadata schema can approximate stakeholder-based metadata schema access, if they permit field-level access permissions. For example, people in Marketing have access to certain fields, while those in Facilities can access other fields.

The advantage that true support for adaptive schemas provides is the flexibility to add or remove "classes" of metadata fields on a per-asset basis, without having to affect the entire system.

Using the example above, adaptive schemas would enable you to add the "Facilities" fields only to the content of interest to that department. There would be no reason to have those fields on, say, budgeting documents or logos. In single-schema content systems, the fields would be added to all content, regardless of type or purpose. This would understandably confuse Marketing employees who, when searching for a logo to place a layout, see fields for "Square Footage" and "Exterior Paint Color Code."

The other side of the multiple metadata schema discussion involves a single piece of content being referenced by multiple systems. In this case, it's expected that each system would have its own metadata schema, perhaps augmenting metadata provided by the source.

The concept of linked content is actually very useful, though in limited practice today. Consider all those "media resources" sections of websites. Here, we can find logos and other standard materials an organization wants to make available to others.

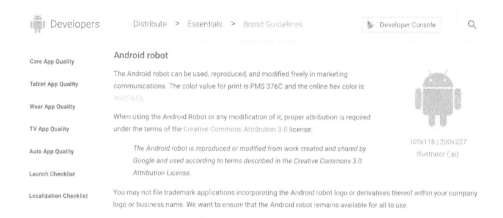

Android robot

The Android robot can be used, reproduced, and modified freely in marketing communications. The color value for print is PMS 376C and the online hex color is #A4C639.

When using the Android Robot or any modification of it, proper attribution is required under the terms of the Creative Commons Attribution 3.0 license:

The Android robot is reproduced or modified from work created and shared by Google and used according to terms described in the Creative Commons 3.0 Attribution License.

You may not file trademark applications incorporating the Android robot logo or derivatives thereof within your company logo or business name. We want to ensure that the Android robot remains available for all to use.

Core App Quality
Tablet App Quality
Wear App Quality
TV App Quality
Auto App Quality
Launch Checklist
Localization Checklist

100x118 | 200x237
Illustrator (.ai)

Google provides a handy website page for those who need access to the Android logo.

Google provides the page above as a means for helping others use the Android logo in an approved, consistent manner. For convenience, they offer a download link to the logo itself and they provide some usage restrictions and other metadata they believe will help others use the logo in compliance with Google policy.

The problem with this approach comes when millions of copies of the Android logo get into circulation. The image below, taken from a Google Image search for "android logo," shows the problem.

Which logo is the current Android logo?

Years of uncontrolled distribution of the Android logo have led to a plethora of variations that make it difficult to know which are official and current.

If instead of making the little robot available as a download, Google might one day make it available only as linked content. Then, from whatever system we use (assuming it supports linked content), we could create a reference to that master content. With that connection, we'd get those usage guidelines we see today on the website. Even better, when those guidelines or the logo itself are updated, we'd see those updates, without having to think about going back to the Google website.

Content linking is actually not such a radical idea. When was the last time you tried to download a YouTube video in order to upload it to Facebook? No one does this. Instead, we link to the original content on YouTube. In part this is because YouTube (wisely) offers no download option; but it's also because videos are large, so moving them around doesn't appeal to us.

Layered over the metadata provided by the original publisher of the master content would be metadata we add that's relevant to our purposes for the logo.

Revisiting the Android logo example, some of our added metadata fields might be:

- Products we sell on the Android platform that use the logo
- Website pages where we have linked the logo

- Advertising campaigns in which we've used the logo

The advantage here would be that when Google updates the logo or its usage guidelines, we have a convenient list of places to check to ensure we're still in compliance with the updated guidelines.

Here are two other examples where linked content provides benefits:

- Government forms that are referenced from multiple locations – By linking to a master version, we know we always have the most recent version.
- Copyrighted materials that are *not* available for distribution but *are* available for linking – Today we think of copyright in terms of "you may or may not possess this." But possession isn't the future of content use. We will need a means for extending "linking" rights that do not include "possession" rights.

It's not uncommon for organizations to link to master content today using website URLs, but this isn't the same thing. A website link provides no metadata, and it affords the "borrowing" organization no means to provide a metadata layer of its own.

So, for example, you might be able to link to the Android logo from your website, but this doesn't help your design department stay informed about usage changes Google might one day publish. And it doesn't help your Product Management department remember which of your products include that logo.

What's more, a proper content link in the future might provide the publisher with a means for proactively notifying those who have linked the content about changes. (Marketers are at this point thinking, "Wow, this could be a killer new way to target advertising!")

The Value of SME Verification and Opinion

Earlier, we talked about how subject matter experts could be used to provide metadata values. We also talked about how a bogus SME's opinion could detract from the value of metadata.

Of course, "bogus" could be subjective. And this is a good thing.

Much like multiple metadata schemas enable different stakeholders to see only the metadata that matters to them, an SME's opinion could mean more to some users than others.

We can address this using a concept similar to "follows" on social media. If you find someone to be of interest, you "follow" that person. Social media engines then, in theory, prioritize postings from that person in your own feed.

Imagine the same concept with content system search results. The contributions of people whom you "follow" get ranked higher in your search results than those you don't. The concept is simple: If you like someone, chances are, you might like to see what that person has to say.

We can extend the benefit of this concept by introducing a weighting scale that extends from the positive into the negative. Whom do you like and whom do you dislike? And how much?

In its most basic form, SME weighting would work like this:

1. You search for assets rated "5" for quality.
2. The system prioritizes content rated "5" by those whose opinions you have indicated you trust. Conversely, content rated "5" by those you have indicated a dislike for would be de-ranked.

The concept can also extend to suggestions. If someone you follow has just marked a new piece of content as "must see," then perhaps you must see it. If it were not for the system suggesting the content to you, you might have never seen it.

People you follow could be those you admire, your boss, your art director or anyone else whose opinion influences (or should influence) your work.

The aggregate of an entire user base could also influence search results. For example, if 95% of a system's user base indicates that a given SME is a genius, the system might universally prioritize that person's opinions. This would be one way of (in theory) increasing search value to users who are new or who have not indicated preferences with regard to SMEs.

In a way, this is how Google Search works. Websites that Google has determined provide more value are ranked higher. (The algorithm for determining results ranking is a closely guarded secret and, in many cases, yields debatable results.)

The importance of this for content management is the same as it is for Google: When the amount of content available becomes overwhelming, you must somehow make it digestible. Google indexes the majority of the Internet and returns 10 options at a time for any given query. In that world, results ranking is everything.

If your content system has only a few thousand pieces of content, ranking might not be as important. For example, if someone searches for "what's new," returning helpful results isn't rocket science if your organization adds only 10 new pieces of content to the system each week.

But what happens if thousands of pieces of content get added to your system every day? The system knowing what you like would then be more than a *good* thing; it would be necessary.

While it's true that some so-called subject matter experts don't actually know as much as they let on, the concept of respect for one's opinion is a powerful feature when it comes to prioritization, in life and in search results.

Imagine how much more useful Google Search would be to you if you were able to indicate which sites hold no interest for you. Never again would you see fan pages for Paris Hilton while trying to make reservations at the Hilton in Paris, and you'd be able to de-rank all those "built for SEO" websites that provide absolutely no value, yet have tricked Google into thinking they are somehow worthwhile.

Come to think of it, why isn't Google actively soliciting our opinions on the results it returns for any given query? We know search results are influenced by what Google thinks we like; now it's time to influence them by what we don't like.

I think about things like this when users of digital asset management and other content management systems ask vendors to make their search work more like Google. "Google-like" search is absolutely not what these systems need.

Everything becomes a Linked Object

If you were at all confused early on in this book about the differences between taxonomy and metadata, that's a good thing. It means your brain was already starting to question a "human made" content management distinction that serves little purpose.

Here's another brain teaser:

What's the difference between metadata and content?

Most would say that metadata describes the content. After all, that's the premise upon which this and other books are based.

But this isn't the whole story. Here's a simple example:

What color is a tangerine?

> Orange

What is "orange"?

> It's a color made of 100% red, 50% green and 0% blue.

How do you say "orange" in Russian?

> Оранжевый

Which international companies feature orange prominently in their logos?

FedEx, Harley Davidson

It turns out that "orange" has attributes of its own. And, again, depending on use case, those different attributes could provide some value.

Say you're working on new branding for Italy's Ducati motorcycle company and you want to vet some color ideas. Fortunately, before going too far with a deep orange you think could be perfect, you see that the color is associated with a formidable Ducati competitor.

Of course there is no one at the Ducati company unfamiliar with Harley-Davidson or its logo colors. But companies often employ outsourced talent who have no understanding of clients' competitive landscapes.

In fact, "orange" is an object, no different than all the "normal" objects in your system that you might tag with "orange." Granted, the color orange is not a physical object. But then, content management is not about managing physical objects.

Taking that example further, though "FedEx" and "Harley Davidson" are attributes of "orange," each of these objects would, in turn, have a wealth of attributes all their own.

Before long, you see how everything is linked to everything else.

Most content systems, however, still don't offer functionality that supports this concept of universal linking. Expect that to change.

Now consider a more complex example involving controlled vocabularies. As mentioned, a controlled vocabulary is a preconfigured list of terms that can be assigned as attributes to describe something in your system. A list of the world's countries is one example.

You're probably already imagining now how each country in that list would have a wealth of attributes.

When you add "Canada" as the location of a photo in your system, what are you indirectly saying about the content?

- The photo was taken in the western hemisphere
- The photo was taken at a northern longitude
- The photo was taken in North America
- The photo was taken in country that speaks English and French
- The photo was taken in a country that is not landlocked
- The photo was taken in a country rich with oil reserves

Who cares, you might wonder, about facts like these and countless others you could add to the "Canada" object. All anyone cares about, you reckon, is where the photo was taken.

Say you add the "Canada" tag to a photo of a Canadian glacier. Let's also say that your content system doesn't support tags that have their own attributes. So, in this case, "Canada" is just a vocabulary term that offers no deeper meaning.

Now, say you need to find photos of glaciers located in regions where French is spoken. You're designing a "save the glaciers" campaign poster for French-speaking regions, so you want to make sure the visual is relevant to your audience.

How would you find this?

You might search for "glacier France," thinking that would find what you need. But there are glaciers in Canada and Switzerland too, and French is widely spoken in both those countries. So while "glacier France" might find glaciers in France, it wouldn't show you everything.

But if you could search for "glaciers *French*," you might find much more when using a systems that supports attributes on tags. Indirectly, you'd see results for photos from Canada, Switzerland and France, because all three countries speak French and all three countries have glaciers.

Chances are, no one would think to add the "French" language tag to photos of glaciers. So, unless your system supported metadata as "objects" that each have their own attributes, this would be a virtually impossible search. (You'd likely have to do some pre-research on Google to figure out which countries have glaciers and, then, which of those countries speak French.)

So, not only do you now have all the glacier images you need, organized by location, you might have also learned about areas of the world that speak French and have glaciers.

Today's search experiences are largely based upon the concept of searching for what we know we have, or at least what we understand in concept. In the future, systems will get better about inferring a goal from a user's search query so that results can be educational as well as handy.

And it will all be based on linking metadata values to derive relationships and relevance.

Algorithms vs. Education

When we speak of a computer inferring meaning from our actions or situations, we most typically mean that some algorithm is working in the background to make connections between bits of information known to it.

For example, if Google knows I'm a son and it knows that Kate is my mother, it could serve ads to me in the week prior to Mother's Day reminding me, "Don't forget about Kate!"

Though perhaps spooky to behold, this isn't difficult to understand. This is simply how algorithmic computing works.

The more complete the available data, or the more of it considered in a given calculation, the more magical the results can appear to us. For example, if Google saw on my mother's calendar that she was having lunch on Mother's Day with her sister, Pat, the ad I see could read, "Give Kate something to brag to Pat about over lunch on Sunday."

By understanding how multiple data points have been considered, the ad becomes less amazing. (Except for the idea that Google would think I would plan anything for Mother's Day more than a few hours in advance of actually seeing my mother. I expect Google to know better.)

In a sense, this is how we're seeing linked data in content systems today, and in the near future. We figure we can tag the entire planet and let the computers infer and present magic from those tags.

But we have room to grow from there.

When we think of metadata today, we think in terms of words. We apply "orange" to the photo of the tangerine, and we might even think about extended tags that apply to orange. But we continue to think in terms of tags being only words or phrases.

But metadata doesn't need to be just simple words, abstracted from any meaning that's not provided by tags assigned to tags.

"Don't stick your finger into the light socket" is among the first lessons taught to a kid. Upon hearing it enough, a kid might actually learn to not stick his finger into a light socket. But the kid who learns this *best* will be the one who actually receives an electrical shock. Suddenly, the meaning of the warning becomes associated with personal experience.

Later in life, when that kid finds himself needing to change his car battery, there will be a respect for the process that someone who has never been shocked wouldn't likely have. In fact, if you've ever been shocked by anything, you can recall that feeling right now.

How is this "life lesson" not metadata on the object that is you?

There are no words to describe the feeling of being shocked, just as there are no tags that could explain that sensation to a computer.

You might have seen a "pain scale" chart when visiting a doctor's office. On the 0 end is "no pain," typically depicted by a happy face. On the 10 end of the chart is "worst pain," depicted by a crying sad face. In the middle of the chart are varying degrees of happy face reduction.

I can't help but wonder about these charts when I see them. Would the "worst pain" imaginable really be where tears would start? I'm sort of thinking that the worst pain possible would render me unconscious, perhaps leaving the flow of tears to start around 7 or 8.

Kudos to the medical community for trying to make a concept as personal as pain something that can be measured. But I wonder about the efficacy of this.

When I'm asked to indicate on the chart how badly something hurts, I find myself considering the outcome of what I say more than I am able to find the perfect face that represents my own. Will I seem like a wimp if I aim too high? Will my concerns be dismissed if I aim too low?

Pain is one object that's tough to tag; heartbreak is another; so is the feeling of electrical shock.

Electrical shock is one type of pain; heartbreak is another type of pain. Despite being related in terms of semantics, psychologists don't ask patients grieving from the loss of a loved one to point at pain scale charts.

Some "values" can be measured only from personal experience.

Given that content systems offer no "personal experience" data field type, it would seem that simple tagging would be the best we could do, in terms of providing a complete metadata profile for our content. And, while relying exclusively on word-based tags, this is just about the best we can do.

But what about the concept of *education as metadata*?

Imagine a team of metadata editors in the future not just assigning tags, but describing concepts to the content system.

Example lessons for the system to learn:

- Glacier photos are relevant to the concept of global warming.
- The artist Prince is not from a royal family.
- "Supermarket" doesn't mean it's better than other markets.

- "Who's your daddy" doesn't always mean the same as "name your father."

Life lessons like these are not specifically taught to us. We come to understand these "truths" based on our ability to connect observations of the world to our understandings of actual facts. Content systems can't do this, and it's not something we could expect in the near future.

But think about search relevance: "I need a photo to illustrate the concept of global warming." Today's systems would be limited to showing you only the content that has been tagged with "global warming" or, perhaps, if wisely added as a synonym, "climate change." But the systems cannot reason to make suggestions based on derived meaning.

"Most popular prince" when searched on Google shows nothing on the first page of results that has anything to do with an actual prince. By contrast, "most popular princess" shows Cinderella, which might make more sense if Cinderella was an actual person.

As impressed as we are with the content technologies available to us, we make allowances where we should not, and we complain about shortcomings in many of the wrong places.

Summary

Metadata and taxonomy enable us to provide the context that is needed to enable our content systems to return relevant search results. They are, in fact, crutches we are forced to use until such time that computers can derive even more meaningful understanding on their own.

In the meantime, keep in mind that designing metadata schemas is not just about enabling users to adequately describe content; it's about anticipating the ways in which users will try to find that content. Add misspellings as synonyms, and consider using tags from popular culture, even if they go against everything you stand for as a linguist or information professional.

Think in terms of multiple metadata schemas so that you're not forced to work with a lowest common denominator schema that only *sort of* works for all user groups.

Don't try to use today's content systems to educate your user base, but expect tomorrow's systems to take on a more active role as educators.

Taxonomies and metadata schemas are nothing more than human/machine interfaces that enable people to find the content they need the moment they need it. Users won't think about why things work or why they don't work; but they will notice and remember both situations for a very long time.

There's nothing you need to know about taxonomy or metadata for content management that you haven't read in this book or can learn on the Web. Forget the academic discussions. If it's your job to make the content system work, then go get started. You'll be far sooner limited by the systems themselves than by the limitations of your own understanding. So don't feel intimidated.

And when you learn what works and doesn't work, write about it so that others can learn from your experience.

Thanks and Next Steps

I started working in the field of Digital Asset Management in 1998. In that time, there have been a few people who have been regular sources of inspiration, information and friendship to me.

David Riecks is a force for DAM industry goodness that cannot be swayed. His ControlledVocabulary.com website was where my education on the subject began. No matter what question I ask him, he gives me answers I didn't even know I needed. There is always something new to learn from David Riecks.

John Horodyski shares my passion for content management to the point where I know people make fun of both of us. Still, a conversation with John is one part information and one part imagination. We see content management that doesn't yet exist. And sometimes, we just get on the phone and vent. I appreciate him for all of it.

Real Story Group is an analyst firm that specializes in enterprise software technologies, like Digital Asset Management and Content Management. Unlike some of their competitors, these people appear to care about the experiences of their customer subscribers. They haven't always been on my side of arguments, but they've always come from a position I can respect.

There's a group of voices in the DAM and Content Management communities who are speaking with authority and integrity. Collectively, they are helping drown the marketing-driven voices of opportunism and ignorance, of which there are plenty. For their contributions in this regard, I thank Deb Fanslow, Lisa Grimm, Tracy Wolfe, Carol Thomas-Knipes, Ian Matzen, Tim Strehle, Romney Whitehead, Holly Boerner, Peter Graham, Jeff Lawrence, Heidi Quicksilver, Emily Kolvitz, Demian Hess, Corey Chimko and, with special appreciation for his inability to succumb to bullshit, Ralph Windsor.

There's a coffee house in Truckee, California called Tuff Beanz. They put up with me while I wrote this book. As my friend and shop owner Mick put it each time he walked in and saw me taking up one of his tables, "Oh look, it's you again." Thanks to Mick, Chris, Judy, Kyle, Amalia, Spencer and Donna for great coffee and kindness.

Across town in a gym called *Performance Trainer Center* is a guy named Jeffrey Graham. Despite my obsession with DQ Blizzards, trainer Jeffrey patiently kicks my ass almost daily to keep me in shape. Two more, Jeffrey! Two more!

When designer Michael P. McHugh saw my original cover design for the book, he insisted that he be permitted to "fix it." Whatever you like was my idea; whatever you don't like was his idea.

When I told Picturepark CEO Ramon Forster about my idea for this book, my hope was only that he wouldn't see it as being in conflict with my day job as the company's marketing director. Instead, he insisted that I take whatever time I needed to make it happen because he considered the topic too important to the community for Picturepark to not support. If Picturepark would focus less on educating and otherwise strengthening the DAM community, it might be better able to focus more on selling DAM software. But I can't think of a single person at the company who would support that idea. Thanks to all my Picturepark coworkers.

The (ever increasing) membership of DAM Guru Program has defied the odds and built themselves into a global content management community that spans all industries, interests, areas of expertise and vendor affiliations. They have become a self-supporting group of professionals who have taught one another, learned from one another, helped one another find jobs and more. Creating DAM Guru Program is, without a doubt, the most important thing I've done for the community. In turn, the membership has never once left me feeling it wasn't absolutely worth the effort. Thanks to all DAM Guru Program members for their dedication to the program and to one another. (And thanks to Picturepark for continuing to pay for it all.)

Speaking of DAM Guru Program, if you're not already a member, there's a free membership waiting for you: http://DAMGuru.com

About the Author

 David Diamond has worked in the field of Digital Asset Management since 1998. His previous book, *DAM Survival Guide*, is considered by many industry gurus to be a must-read for those new to the field.

In 2013, Diamond created DAM Guru Program, now the world's largest community of digital asset and content management professionals. In the same year, he was awarded the "DAMMY of the Year," the industry's highest honor, for his contributions to content management education.

Diamond has held senior management positions at Apple, Sony and the University of Southern California. He is an accomplished 3D illustrator and author for Aviation audiences, and a licensed pilot.

Diamond co-founded, recorded and toured with the 80s band Berlin.

He now lives in Truckee, California, from where he directs global community education and marketing for Swiss software maker, Picturepark.

Diamond's first two books, *Flight Training: Taking the Short Approach* and *DAM Survival Guide,* are available from Amazon and other booksellers.

Contact the author:

david@ContentManagementBook.com

linkedin.com/in/airdiamond

Twitter: @DAMSurvival

Stay connected at: ContentManagementBook.com

www.ingramcontent.com/pod-product-compliance
Lightning Source LLC
Chambersburg PA
CBHW080414060326
40689CB00019B/4240